AIKIDO

In Training

AIKIDO
In Training

A Manual of Traditional Aikido Practice & Principles

R. Crane-5th Dan
K. Crane-5th Dan

COOL RAIN PRODUCTIONS
BERLIN, NEW JERSEY

Published by
Cool Rain Productions
P.O. Box 145
Berlin, New Jersey 08009
U.S.A.

ISBN 0-9636429-5-2
Library of Congress Catalog Card Number: 93-71042

Library of Congress Cataloging-in-Publication Data
Crane, R.
    Aikido in training: a manual of traditional Aikido
practice and principles / by R. Crane and K.Crane. - 1st ed.
    336 p. : illus. ; 14 cm.
    ISBN 0-9636429-5-2
    1. Aikido. I. Crane, K. II. Title.
GV1114.35.C72   1993
796.8154 dc20   93-71042

WARNING

This book in not intended as a substitute for personal supervised instruction.
The Publisher and the Authors will not be held responsible in any way whatsoever
for any physical injury, or damage of any kind, which may result from the reader(s)
following the instruction therein. Therefore, it is essential that before attempting any of
the exercises and or techniques described in this book, that the
reader(s) should consult a qualifed physician to ascertain their physical ability
to engage in the activities depicted in this book, and the reader(s) should seek qualified
and competent personal instruction.

Dedicated in Loving Memory
to the Blessed Souls of
Shelob and **Rhoda**

Special thanks to:

Robert J. Paull Jr. for technical photographs.

Stanley Pranin, Editor-in-Chief Aiki-News, for many of the photos of O'Sensei.

Donna Reed for photo preparation and cover design.

Donata Brown for proofing text.

Frank McAleer for computer support.

Ukemi:

Paul Padula San-Dan

Regis A. Yurcich San-Dan

Jane Shaw San-Dan

Gene Ford Ni-Dan

Donna Reed Sho-Dan

Michael T. Pellegrino Sho-Dan

Jason Zimmer Sho-Dan

O'SENSEI UESHIBA MORIHEI 1883 - 1969
Founder of AIKIDO

TABLE OF CONTENTS

FOREWORD *9*

INTRODUCTION *11*

BIOGRAPHY: "FOUNDER OF AIKIDO - O'SENSEI, UESHIBA MORIHEI" *13*

PRINCIPLES OF TRAINING: "OBSERVATIONS ON" *25*

METHODS OF TRAINING *41*

AIKI-SHISEI: "POSTURES OF AIKIDO" *41*

TAI-NO HENKO: "BODY CHANGING" *49*

KOKYU RYOKU TAISO: "BREATH POWER - EXERCISE" *49*

SABAKI TAISO: "BODY TURNING - EXERCISE" *57*

UKEMI: "THE ART OF RECEIVING" *65*

SHIKKO: "KNEE WALKING" *65*

KOGEKI: "TERMINOLOGY OF ATTACKS" *65*

KATAME WAZA: "TECHNIQUES OF IMMOBILIZATION" *75*

TAI-JUTSU: "BODY ARTS" *81*

IKKYO: "FIRST TEACHING" *83*

NIKYO: "SECOND TEACHING" *93*

SANKYO: "THIRD TEACHING" *105*

YONKYO: "FOURTH TEACHING" *115*

GOKYO: "FIFTH TEACHING" *123*

SHIHO-NAGE: "FOUR DIRECTION THROW" *129*

KOTEGAESHI: "WRIST TURN" *143*

KAITEN-NAGE: "ROTARY THROW" *155*

KOSHI-NAGE: "HIP THROW" *163*

TENCHI-NAGE: "HEAVEN-EARTH THROW" *173*

CONTINUED ☞

TAI-JUTSU: "BODY ARTS" continued

AIKI-OTOSHI: "AIKI DROP" *179*

SUMI-OTOSHI: "CORNER DROP" *179*

AIKI-NAGE: "AIKI THROW" *179*

JUJI-GARAMI: "CROSS ENTWINING TECHNIQUE" *187*

IRIMI-NAGE: "ENTERING THROW" *193*

KOKYU-NAGE: "BREATH THROW" *207*

HIJI WAZA: "ELBOW TECHNIQUE" *223*

GANSEKI-OTOSHI: "HEELS OVER HEAD DROP" *233*

MEN-NAGE: "HEAD THROW" *233*

TANTO-TORI: "KNIFE TAKING" *243*

HANMI-HANDACHI WAZA: "HALF-BODY HALF-STANDING TECHNIQUES" *257*

SUWARI WAZA: "SEATED TECHNIQUES" *271*

HENKA WAZA: "VARIED TECHNIQUES" *287*

KAESHI WAZA: "COUNTER TECHNIQUES" *287*

JIYU/RANDORI WAZA: "FREE STYLE / VARIED ATTACK" *287*

BUKI WAZA: "WEAPON TECHNIQUES" *297*

AIKI-KEN: "AIKI SWORD" *299*

AIKI-JO: "AIKI STAFF" *315*

GLOSSARY: *329*

JAPANESE KANJI APPEARING IN TABLE OF CONTENTS
*This page: **DOJO** - "Way Place"*
*Previous page: **AGATSU** - "Self Victory"*

FOREWORD

In the Aikido world today there is a widespread tendency toward simplification of the technical system of the art and emphasis on the more advanced level known as *Ki no Nagare* or "*Ki* flow" techniques. As a result, the richness and depth of the Aiki techniques passed on to posterity by Aikido Founder Morihei Ueshiba have become considerably diluted. Particularly absent is a stress on the importance of basic techniques for beginning level students.

In light of this situation, this new book *Aikido In Training* by professional instructors Richard and Kathy Crane represents a significant step toward a reversal of this trend. The Cranes place a strong emphasis on the correct performance of basic techniques which is essential for advancement to higher skill levels attainable only through long years of assiduous training. Their approach follows a logical progression from basic to applied techniques for the more advanced practitioner. Moreover, due attention is given to the often neglected area of Aiki weapons. *Aikido In Training* contains hundreds of photographs and lucid explanations which take the reader to a much deeper level of understanding far beyond what one might of the typical "How to" book on martial arts.

In summary, those contemplating the study of traditional Aikido or who are already students of the "Aiki Way" will find in this book an invaluable tool for understanding the subtleties of this unique Japanese martial art.

Stanley Pranin

Editor-in-Chief, AIKI NEWS

Tokyo, April 26, 1993

"All the secret teachings
        are to be found in the simple basics"

O'Sensei Ueshiba Morihei

INTRODUCTION

Aikido is solely the creation of *Ueshiba Morihei*. *Aikido In Training* is a humble attempt to illustrate and explain some of the fundamental practice and principles of the art of this great man. Our hope is that it will stimulate both beginner and advanced students to intensify their endeavor on the path of *Aiki* as well as demonstrate the basis of Traditional *Aikido* training to all who turn its pages.

This book has been laid out and written so that each technique depicted seeks to demonstrate the proper position and interrelationship of hands, feet, hips, etc. in a step by step manner. The use of wording such as "forceful" or "powerfully" is by no means inadvertent; instead, it is meant to imply the active use of Body, Mind, and Spirit during the application of the martial principles of *Aikido*. Of course, the most intricate subtleties can be transmitted only through direct instruction from teacher to student; therefore, this book should be used as a complement to direct instruction, not in lieu of it.

Within the text, Japanese names appear in the traditional manner of family name before first name. In the biographic section, the respectful term *O'Sensei* has been used rather than *Morihei*, even when describing his adolescent years. Also, throughout this book, the term *Aiki-Deshi* (student of *Aikido*) has been used in place of the overused term *Aikidoka* (practitioner of *Aikido*, one of high rank).

It is important to note that there is no competition in the Traditional *Aikido* of *O'Sensei*; it is not a sport, nor is it a hobby, a trend, or a religion. Rather, it is a pure *Budo* (Martial Way), developed and endowed by *O'Sensei* with the principles of loving protection for all things, recognizing that we all share an undeniable connection with the totality of the universe.

The *Aikido* of *O'Sensei Ueshiba Morihei* is a *Budo* which demands we face and deal with the pettiness and barriers within; developing the strength to prevail and strive toward our higher personal potential.

GAMBATTE !

R. Crane K. Crane

Dojo-Cho Agatsu Dojos

New Jersey, USA

FOUNDER of AIKIDO
" O'SENSEI UESHIBA MORIHEI "

" Background, Development, and Evolution of Aikido "

PROLOGUE:

Constructed with the intention of conveying a correct and unexaggerated account of the history of *O'Sensei Ueshiba Morihei*, it is hoped that this section will assist in bringing the reader to a clearer understanding of the background and development of *Aikido*. Please note that the Japanese names appearing throughout the text of this book are respectfully in the traditional configuration of last name preceding first name. Though painstakingly researched, any error which may arise within this text is solely that of the author.

INTRODUCTION:

The late eighteen hundreds found Japan in a state of rapid transition. Though embracing a deep sense of national pride and heritage, Japan found itself caught up in the desire to develop as a country of economic freedom and power such as was evident in Europe and America. Though in the rural areas traditional garments and lifestyles were still the mainstay, it was not uncommon to see an abundance of western clad individuals strolling the streets of downtown *Tokyo* and other metropolitan areas.

Having been persuaded (in 1854) by the presence of the United States Navy under the command of Commodore Perry, Japan had ended its self-imposed isolation with the signing of the *Kanagawa* Treaty. The Japanese government had then begun, through the strong recommendations of the military, to develop a powerful modern military force, a force which from time to time was permitted to display its teeth within the Asian hemisphere. While, at least on the surface, the divisions of classes within the structure of society had for the most part disappeared, it can be said that the *Bushi* (*samurai*) had all but vanished. Many of the traditional *Bujutsu* (martial art/science) were facing extinction, due mostly to lack of interest by the general public and the military's focus on sheer fire power as opposed to the individual warrior's martial expertise.

Japan was no different from most other countries as it approached the turn of the century, yet it was still uniquely Japan. It was during this turbulent period filled with its share of adversity, prosperity, hardship, and hope that *O'Sensei Ueshiba Morihei* was born.

TANABE: 1883 to 1912

Born in the town of *Tanabe* in *Kii* Province (now *Wakayama* Prefecture) on December 14, 1883, *Ueshiba Morihei* was the only son of *Yoroku* and *Yuki*. Involved in fishing and lumber operations, *O'Sensei's* father *Yoroku* (1843-1920), a prosperous area landowner, was said to be a very powerfully built individual with some background in the martial arts, possibly *Kito-Ryu Jujutsu*. It is easy to believe that *O'Sensei* must have received special affection as *Yoroku's* only son, and it seems naturally fitting that *Yoroku* would have wanted his son to grow up to take over his hard-earned business ventures. But it should be noted that even when *O'Sensei* came of age and his aspirations were directed toward other areas, *Yoroku* was always supportive of his son's decisions.

From an early age *O'Sensei* proved to be notably adept in mathematics, an interest which was to prove helpful in his first business ventures. Apparently, as a youth *O'Sensei* was not very physically active; in fact, it seems he experienced his fair share of adolescent diseases. *O'Sensei* studied the nine volumes of the Chinese Classics under the direction of *Fujimoto Mitsujo*, a priest of the *Jizoji* Temple located near the *Ueshiba* home in *Tanabe*. Mathematics, the Chinese Classics, and the reading of books about ancient Japanese culture and *Shinto* seem to have taken the place of excessive youthful roughhousing.

Though no one is really sure what one event, if any, was the true turning point in his outlook toward physical training, clearly once the desire took hold, *O'Sensei's* devotion to his personal development became absolute. Upon finishing studies at the *Yoshida* Institute, a school of higher mathematics, *O'Sensei* worked at a local tax office before venturing out on his own to *Tokyo* at the tender age of seventeen.

While running a small stationery supply business in *Tokyo*, he took up the practice of *Tenjin Shin'yo-Ryu Jujutsu* (1) under *Tozawa Tokusaburo* (1848-1912) and possibly for a short period studied *Shinkage-Ryu* sword at the *Idabashi Dojo*. Returning to *Tanabe* after a bout with beriberi, *O'Sensei* married *Itogawa Hatsu* (1881-1969) and shortly thereafter joined the Army Infantry at the age of nineteen. Involved by that time in the severe training of his body, *O'Sensei* was immediately noted as a powerful physical presence in his regiment. Furthermore, his background in the martial arts as well as his training in the *Goto-Ha* school of *Yagyu Shingan-Ryu Jujutsu* (lasting from 1903 to 1908) seem to have gained the attention of his superiors, and he was promptly given the task of assisting in the martial arts training of his fellow soldiers. During his time in the service, *O'Sensei* served on the Manchurian front in the Russo-Japanese War and was said to have shown extraordinary resolve in the face of combat.

Following his discharge from the Army, *O'Sensei* returned to his home town of *Tanabe* and continued his relentless personal training. Wishing to find a way to test and push himself even harder, *O'Sensei* traveled to Japan's northern-most island of *Hokkaido* to explore the possibility of developing the inhospitable land often noted for its Siberian-like winters. Finding the challenge to be to his liking, in 1912 at the age of twenty-eight, *O'Sensei* obtained the approval of the government to lead a large group of settlers consisting of over fifty families to the *Monbetsu* area of *Hokkaido*.

DAITO-RYU and the OMOTO-KYO: 1912 to 1931

"Great things arise from great hardship" was to prove to be a true maxim in the lives of the settlers under *O'Sensei's* guidance. Founded in May of 1912, the village of *Shirataki* in *Monbetsu* county was to be the home of the relocated families from *Wakayama*, as well as a small number of other independent settlers. The first three years brought adversities which were most likely beyond the expectations of even *O'Sensei*. Farming of the newly open land proved difficult, and food as well as shelter was sparse.

As attempts at farming failed year after year, the arduous work of clearing the land of its seemingly countless number of trees was to prove a means of salvation in disguise. Through the guidance of *O'Sensei*, the villagers were able to sell lumber in order to buy food and the bare essentials for survival. It has been written that during this period *O'Sensei* was as a man possessed, doing the work of ten men, laboring from sunup to sundown seven days a week, always the first one to pitch in, helping whenever and whomever he could. Tireless in his efforts to succeed, *O'Sensei* appeared to have found a way to fully blend his desire to help others with that of his personal training. Clearly, *O'Sensei* was instrumental in the founding, development, and survival of *Shirataki*. Today in *Shirataki* there stands a monument in memory of the founder of *Aikido, O'Sensei Ueshiba Morihei*.

Toward the end of the third year, life in the village began to stabilize. The crops which had been so poor in previous years began to yield a reliable harvest, and the newly established lumber business was proving fruitful. Though these positive events must have given great joy to the now thirty-one-year-old *O'Sensei*, it can be stated without doubt that his meeting with the famous *Takeda Sokaku* in the *Hisada* Inn was the most significant.

Having heard that a great master of *Jujutsu* was staying in the town of *Engaru, Hokkaido,* *O'Sensei* was able to gain an introduction through the help of *Yoshida Kotaro,* a fellow avid martial arts practitioner. *Takeda Sokaku* (1860-1943), the headmaster of *Daito-Ryu Jujutsu,* was said to be a man of formidable appearance even though he stood only a little over four feet eleven inches tall. *Takeda Sensei* traveled extensively, teaching *Daito-Ryu* to members of the police, military officers, judges, and other well-to-do persons throughout Japan. In view of this rather elite list of students, *Takeda Sensei* undoubtedly accepted *O'Sensei* as a personal student due to *O'Sensei's* sincerity of heart as well as his impressive physical presence.

Over the course of his lifetime *O'Sensei* both trained in and mastered numerous traditional martial arts of Japan, but it is clear that the *Daito-Ryu* of *Takeda Sokaku* was to have the most profound effect on the technical aspects of the development of *Aikido.* The documented relationship of *O'Sensei's* exposure to *Daito-Ryu* spans a period lasting from his first encounter in 1915 through April of 1931, though it is said that his involvement with *Takeda Sensei* continued until 1937. During the time in which *O'Sensei* was part of the *Daito-Ryu,* he received the transmission scrolls of *Hiden Mokuroku, Hiden Ogi, Goshi'yo No-Te,* and finally *Kyoju-Dairi,* acting as *Takeda Sensei's* assistant and sometimes teaching in his stead. Unquestionably *O'Sensei Ueshiba Morihei* was among the most distinguished of *Takeda Sensei's* pupils.

O'Sensei, Kobukan Dojo circa 1933

Along with the great efforts made by *Takeda Sokaku,* and in later years his son *Tokimune,* it is believed by many that the emergence of *Aikido* is in some part responsible for the survival of *Daito-Ryu* in the face of the ensuing extinction of so many other *Ryu* (styles).

The year 1920 brought many changes to the life of *O'Sensei.* Turning his land holdings over to his teacher, *Takeda Sokaku, O'Sensei* left much of his personal property behind in *Hokkaido* and made the long journey back to *Tanabe* to be with his desperately ill father, *Yoroku,* only to find his arrival was too late. Deciding to dedicate himself to obtaining a deeper understanding of spiritual matters, *O'Sensei* returned to the small town of *Ayabe,* where he had stopped to pray for his father's recovery on his long trek home from *Hokkaido. Ayabe* was the site of the *Omoto-Kyo,* a relatively new sect of *Shinto* (Japan's native religion). Founded by *Deguchi Nao* (1836-1918), the *Omoto-Kyo* was at that time under the direction of the rather flamboyant personage of *Deguchi Onisaburo* (1871-1948). Drawn to the study of the *Kotodama* (an ancient system of beliefs holding that sounds are at the core of reality and have an intrinsic ability to affect the physical realm), *O'Sensei* once again threw himself wholeheartedly into his practice, becoming a steadfast supporter of *Deguchi.*

It seems *Deguchi* instinctively recognized *O'Sensei's* destiny to be one with *Budo* (martial way), not religion, and was instrumental in *O'Sensei's* decision to establish a *Dojo* in *Ayabe.*

Though the time in which *O'Sensei* stayed in *Ayabe* and studied under *Deguchi* is full of colorful events, there are no two which stand out more than the birth of his third and only surviving son *Kisshomaru* and the opening of the *Ueshiba Juku Dojo* (*Ueshiba* private school of *Jujutsu*). These two events were to mark the beginning of the dissemination of *O'Sensei's* unique approach to the martial arts and their link to the future.

As *O'Sensei's* fame as a martial arts master spread, he was urged by his student and supporter Admiral *Takeshita Isamu* and others to once again move to *Tokyo*. So after seven years in *Ayabe*, *O'Sensei* relocated his family in 1927 to the *Shiba* area of *Tokyo* to open a *Dojo*. In 1931, after moving from one temporary location to another, *O'Sensei* (through the help of funds raised from the sale of land inherited from his father and the support of benefactors) opened a permanent *Dojo* in the *Ushigome, Shinjuku* area of *Tokyo*. Dedicated under the name *Kobukan*, the *Dojo* swiftly earned the nickname "Hell *Dojo*."

AIKI-BUDO ERA: 1931 to 1941

Until 1931 the methods taught by *O'Sensei* were amassed under various titles including *Ueshiba-Ryu Jujutsu*, but the techniques for the most part were those of *Daito-Ryu*. The years of teaching and personal training spent in and around *Ayabe* seem to have generated a feeling in *O'Sensei* that a new martial art was necessary, one with the true virtue of *Budo* as its goal, a goal of a path to self-perfection. *O'Sensei* took the first steps toward this goal with the designation of the name *Aiki-Budo* to signify his art as the *Kobukan* era arrived.

Standing approximately five feet one and one-half inches tall, *O'Sensei* was said to have been one hundred and sixty pounds of muscular intensity and martial expertise. It has been written by a number of the *Uchi-Deshi* (inside/live-in students) of this period that *O'Sensei* was so totally absorbed in his personal training and the development of his way of *Aiki* that to merely attend a training session at that time was an act of courage. Nevertheless, the eighty *Tatami* mats of the *Kobukan* drew many strong young practitioners, and the membership quickly grew even though entry to training was only permitted with a letter of introduction from a proper guarantor. Among the many notable students during the "Hell *Dojo*" period were *Yukawa Tsutomu* (1911-1943), *Yonekawa Shigemi* (1910-), *Inoue Noriaki* (1902-) a nephew of *O'Sensei*, *Tomiki Kenji* (1900-1979), *Shioda Gozo* (1915-), and *Shirata Rinjiro* (1912-).

Though early chronicles of the *Kobukan* are filled with the stuff legends are made of, it should be noted that four tangible records of that period have also been preserved. The first of note is the 1933 publication of a technical manual entitled <u>Budo Renshu</u> (translated, <u>Training in Budo</u>) which depicts over two hundred techniques in the form of line drawings, preceded by *Doka* (long-form poems) of *O'Sensei*. The second is the making of a documentary film in 1935 for the *Osaka Asahi* newspaper, clearly illustrating the pre-war *Aiki-Budo* of *O'Sensei*. The third is the 1938 publication of <u>Budo</u>, a training manual depicting in photographic form some fifty techniques performed by *O'Sensei*. Both books, <u>Budo Renshu</u> and <u>Budo</u>, were printed in limited quantities and presented to both benefactors and students who showed particular aptitude. The last item involves a series of over 1,500 photographs of *O'Sensei* taken in or around 1935 at the *Otsuka Dojo* of *Noma Seiji* (founder of one of Japan's largest publishing companies). Often referred to as the "*Noma Dojo* photos," they are the most comprehensive study of the early foundation techniques of *Aikido*. Regrettably, to date, this extensive set of photos has never been collectively published in its entirety.

As the *Kobukan* flourished, the number of branch *Dojo* grew to include such places as the Naval Staff College and the Military Police School. In 1939 the *Kobukan* was incorporated into the *Kobukai* Foundation for the sake of improving the management and financial aspects of the *Dojo*. This restructuring was to prove beneficial to the reorganization which became necessary following the Second World War. Around the same period, *O'Sensei* made the decision to change from the traditional method of awarding *Mokuroku* (transmission scrolls) to the newer standard of the *Kyu-Dan* system, in this way making student grading more suitable for the future of the art.

The era of the "Hell *Dojo*" came to a close in 1940 as the tensions of the fighting in China steadily drew more and more men to active military duty. Still, in the face of these troubled times the *Kobukan Dojo* continued to attract students of the highest caliber, students such as *Tohei Koichi* (1920-), *Osawa Kisaburo* (1911-1991), and *Hirai Minoru* (1903-).

In 1941 Admiral *Takeshita*, a long time student and staunch supporter of *O'Sensei*, arranged for a demonstration of *Aiki-Budo* to be given for members of Japan's Imperial family. There

has been much written about the events surrounding the demonstration given by *O'Sensei* at the *Sainenkan Dojo* on the grounds of the imperial palace. At the time *O'Sensei* was seriously ill, suffering from a recurring stomach disorder, and could barely walk without assistance. But apparently, once the time of the demonstration came, his performance was so explosive as to render one attacker unable to continue while bringing to the point of total exhaustion his other much younger attacker.

O'Sensei performing Shiho-Nage, Noma Dojo photos 1935

With the chill winds of December 1941 came the beginning of Japan's fateful entry into the Second World War. Now engaged in battles to both the east and west, a great time of change was quickly descending upon Japan, and the *Kobukan Dojo* and the *Aiki-Budo* of *O'Sensei* were not to be exempt from the clutches of this tremendous state of transition.

BIRTH of AIKIDO: 1942 to 1969

The year 1942 is indicated as the year in which the term *Aikido* was first officially used as the name of *O'Sensei's* art. The designation *Aikido* was at that time registered with both the *Dai Nihon Butokukai* and the Ministry of Education. The final transition from the term *Aiki-Budo* to *Aikido* secured a permanent place for the *Budo* of *O'Sensei* within the martial arts of Japan.

As the war took a turn for the worse, it has been said that *O'Sensei* became deeply distressed over the fate of Japan. Though strongly supportive of the Emperor, it seems that *O'Sensei* was quite disturbed by the destructively aggressive strategy adopted by the military in the Pacific theater. So, in 1942 *O'Sensei* retired as the head of the *Kobukan* and moved from *Tokyo* to a small town in *Ibaragi* Prefecture known as *Iwama*. Accompanied by his devoted wife *Hatsu*, *O'Sensei's* aim was to combine his life of *Budo* with that of farming. Secluding himself within the spirituality he found in the arduous task of working the soil, the

O'Sensei, circa 1955

fifty-eight-year-old *O'Sensei* set about the task of realizing his dream of a true and pure form of *Budo*. Dedicated to the purpose of communing with nature, *O'Sensei* chose to name his property in *Iwama* the *Aiki-En* (*Aiki*-farm). This choice was to prove to be inadvertently beneficial to the continuation of *Aikido* during the restrictive period of the post-war restoration of Japan. It is this period of intense training in *Iwama*, which lasted from 1942 to the mid 1950s, that *O'Sensei* most attributed to the birth of modern day *Aikido*.

When *O'Sensei* retired to *Iwama*, he named *Ueshiba Kisshomaru* as director of the *Kobukan Dojo*. The twenty-one-year-old *Kisshomaru* had wholeheartedly devoted himself to training since 1936. The difficult years which followed his appointment as *Kobukan* director earned *Kisshomaru* a position of great respect and appreciation among even the most senior of students. Aside from his ability to maintain the *Dojo* despite a dwindling number of students due to the call to military service, *Kisshomaru* was also single-handedly responsible for saving the *Kobukan Hombu* (home) *Dojo* during the almost nightly bombardment of *Tokyo* toward the end of the war. Time after time throughout the night, *Kisshomaru* hosed down the *Dojo* structure, effectively safeguarding it from the fire storms which claimed most of the surrounding buildings.

In *Iwama*, *O'Sensei* was deeply involved with training in the open air *Dojo* and working on the construction of the *Aiki-Jinja* (*Aiki*-Shrine). Established in 1943 as an *Omoto* shrine, *O'Sensei* installed and dedicated the *Aiki-Jinja* to the *Kami* which he modestly believed to be the source of his development of *Aikido*. The original small wood frame *Jinja*, though no longer in use, still stands behind the larger permanent structure which was completed in or around 1962. To this day on the site of the *Aiki-Jinja* a ceremony and demonstration is held on April 29 of each year to mark the passing of *O'Sensei*.

The end of the war came in August 1945 to a stunned and demoralized Japan. The occupation forces headed by General MacArthur imposed a ban on the practice of all martial arts, save *Karate* which it did not deem threatening. This ban marked the end of a number of arts that had teetered on the edge of extinction even before the war's start. During this part of the occupation, the practice of *Aikido* would have come to a complete standstill had it not been for the efforts of *O'Sensei* at *Iwama*. Due to the ban, the *Kobukan Dojo* was forced to totally suspend training sessions, so the decision was made to move the center of *Aikido* to the *Iwama Dojo*, on which construction had just been completed. Offering the *Dojo* as temporary shelter to as many as thirty displaced and homeless families, *Kisshomaru* moved to *Iwama* where he could once again engage in daily training with his father.

Throughout the entire time the ban on martial arts was in effect, the occupation forces never once investigated the little parcel of land located approximately sixty-five miles northeast of *Tokyo*, with the small sign proudly proclaiming the area to be the *Aiki-En*. This does not mean that *O'Sensei* surreptitiously conducted practice, but it is safe to say there were no fireworks set off to announce training sessions. Even with the situation as it was, many of the older students of *O'Sensei* who had been fortunate enough to survive the war in one piece, were slowly but surely finding their way to *Iwama* to renew their training. Upon their return they were to find a number of new students, such as *Saito Morihiro* and *Abe Tadashi*, earnestly engaged in training.

Finally, in 1948 under the authorization of the Act of Endowment, the *Kobukai* Foundation was reestablished as the *Zaidan Hojin Aikikai*, or the *Aikikai* Foundation as it is most often referred to. This monumental step in the rebirth of *Aikido* on a large scale came about through the tireless efforts of *Kisshomaru* and supporters of *O'Sensei* such as *Fujita Kinya* and *Nishi Katsuzo*. Though the *Aikikai Hombu Dojo* was located in *Iwama* until 1956, daily training resumed at the site of the old *Kobukan Dojo* as early as 1949.

The early 1950s mark the beginning of the spread of *Aikido* to Europe and the United States, with *Mochizuki* traveling to France and *Tohei Koichi* to Hawaii. As training increased in *Tokyo* and *Iwama*, and many of the older *Dojo* reopened and were joined by others in places such as *Kumano* and *Osaka*, *Aikido* was rapidly entering a new age of expansion, a time which was to be called by many "The Golden Age of *Aikido*."

As *Aikido* gained in popularity, *O'Sensei* was drawn more and more from his farming and personal training in *Iwama* to teaching in *Tokyo* and various areas throughout Japan. In 1956 *O'Sensei* finally gave his consent for demonstrations to be given to the general public. The word of his unique art even reached the ears of the media, and in 1958 at the age of seventy-four *O'Sensei* agreed to appear in a documentary short filmed for American television.

With the number of new students growing steadily, *Kisshomaru* was able to leave his part-time job in 1955 and devote his full attention to the *Dojo* in *Tokyo*. Having been given full rein to run the *Aikikai* Foundation as he saw fit, *Kisshomaru* was able to accomplish the task of systematizing, categorizing, and assigning names to many of the techniques which had been taught previously in random order. Under the authority and guidance of *O'Sensei*, *Kisshomaru* published his first book on *Aikido* in 1957. From that time until present, *Kisshomaru* has authored some twenty volumes which have appeared in several languages, most having been published since the passing of *O'Sensei*.

Though *Aikido* was one of the first arts in which women were permitted to train on an equal basis with men, it should be noted that it was not until the mid 1950s that the influx of female students in larger numbers began. The gracious *Sunadomari Fukiko* is a good example of the dedicated and sincere women students of that time.

With the arrival of the 1960s and "The Golden Age of *Aikido*" at its peak, the art of *O'Sensei* which had been developed as a path for the betterment of the individual and subsequently all of mankind, was rapidly drawing a strong following in many foreign countries. By this time, the second, and in some cases third, group of *Uchi-Deshi*

O'Sensei, Iwama Dojo circa 1962

(inside students) were being sent overseas. These *Aikikai* instructors were charged with the task of establishing *Dojo* and assisting in the further development of the already existing non-Japanese instructors. Among those sent abroad during this period were *Tamura Nobuyoshi* to France; *Yamada Yoshimitsu, Maruyama Shuji, Kanai Mitsunari* to the United States; *Tada Hiroshi* to Italy; *Sugano Seiichi* to Australia; and *Chiba Kazuo* to the United Kingdom.

In 1961 *O'Sensei* was to make his first and only trip to the United States. The purpose of the visit was the commemoration of the opening of the newly constructed *Wailea Dojo* in Oahu, Hawaii. Lasting for forty days, the visit allowed for *O'Sensei* to both teach and sightsee throughout the islands.

O'Sensei leading *Keiko* circa 1965

The international spread of *Aikido* also brought a greater recognition of *Aikido* in Japan, with *O'Sensei* receiving "The Medal of Honor with Purple Ribbon" in 1960 and "The Order of the Rising Sun, 4th Class" as the Founder of *Aikido* in 1964. Beginning in 1963 and held each year since, *Aikido* groups from throughout Japan come together for the "All Japan *Aikido* Demonstration" in honor of *O'Sensei's* art.

In the midst of the tremendous growth of the 1960s came the need for a larger headquarters *Dojo*, so plans were launched for the construction of a multi-story structure to be built on the site of the original *Kobukan Dojo*. With the immense efforts of all involved and more than likely a good degree of strain on the home life of *O'Sensei* and his wife *Hatsu*, who were at this point spending most of their time in *Tokyo*, the present *Aikikai Hombu Dojo* was born. Completed in December of 1967 and dedicated to the spirit of *Aiki* on January 12, 1968, the sense of accomplishment of purpose must have, deservedly, been a great one for *O'Sensei*. The spacious four story *Dojo* is to this day a focal point for the spread of *Aikido*, attracting students from virtually all corners of the globe. The year 1968 was truly a magnificent one for *Aikido*, overshadowed only by the gradually failing health of *O'Sensei*.

Attired in a pure white *Keiko-Dogi* and *Hakama* (training uniform), on January 15, 1969, at the age of eighty-five, *O'Sensei* gave his last public demonstration on the occasion of the *Kagami-Biraki* (New Year's Celebration). Fittingly, the demonstration was held at the *Aikikai Hombu Dojo* and attended by students, friends, and supporters. *O'Sensei* had often proclaimed *Takemusu-Aiki* (The spontaneous and prolific creation of technique, one upon another in rapid succession, embodied with the principles of *Aiki*) to be the foremost expression of *Aikido*. The uncompromising demonstration given that day by the frail but proud and upright figure of the Founder, has been described by many as a true manifestation of the essence of *Takemusu-Aiki*. Thanks to its preservation on film this historical footage has been viewed by literally thousands of persons worldwide.

The date of March 10, has been given as the last date on which *O'Sensei* rose to engage in training. His health having been drained by his long bout with liver cancer, *O'Sensei Ueshiba Morihei*, Founder of *Aikido*, passed away in his sleep in the bedroom of his living quarters at the *Hombu Dojo* at 5:00am on April 26, 1969.

The ashes of *O'Sensei* are interred at the *Ueshiba* family burial site in *Tanabe*. Portions of the hair and beard of *O'Sensei* have been preserved at the *Hombu Dojo*, *Iwama Dojo*, *Kumano Dojo*, and in *Ayabe*. To this day, the grave site of *O'Sensei* in *Tanabe* is cared for regularly by students who come to visit and pray for the peaceful repose of this great teacher, a man who created a pure *Budo* of mind, body, and spirit, opening the path to all with the resolve to follow its rigorous journey. Those who come together to train under the name *Aikido* must always remember and pass on the understanding that *O'Sensei*, as the title implies (2), is truly "one who has gone a great distance before."

It is said that one can never truly die unless his memory passes from our hearts. If this is so, and I most vehemently believe it to be, then *O'Sensei Ueshiba Morihei*, a man who has deeply touched the lives of hundreds of thousands, will live forever in the honest endeavor found in the traditional training of *Aikido*.

The DOTO: 1969 to Present

Upon the passing of *O'Sensei*, the position of *Doshu* (way leader) was bestowed upon *Ueshiba Kisshomaru*. The title of *Aikido Doshu* and the formidable task of continuing the dream of *O'Sensei* in the face of a new era, was made even more difficult with the passing of his mother, *Hatsu*. Her mission of caring for *O'Sensei* having been completed, *Ueshiba Hatsu* followed her husband exactly two months to the day, on June 26, 1969. It is safe to say that *O'Sensei's* perseverance and extreme devotion to the path of his *Budo* can only truly be matched by his life-long companion's behind-the-scenes resolve.

Ueshiba Moriteru, grandson of *O'Sensei* and second son of the new *Doshu*, was to later take his place in the order of the *Doto* (system of family succession) as *Waka Sensei* (young teacher) and subsequently in 1986 was designated *Dojo-Cho* (*Dojo* director) of the *Aikikai Hombu Dojo*, securing the lineage of *Aikido* well into the twenty-first century.

1: It is still, even at this point in time, quite impossible to fully and accurately list all the arts with which *O'Sensei* was involved during his lifetime. Therefore, the ones listed within this text are a few of those currently accepted by knowledgeable *Aikido* historians, i.e. *Aikido Doshu Ueshiba Kisshomaru*, and Stanley Pranin (editor-in-chief *Aiki-News* and dedicated *Aikido* researcher for over two decades).

2: See - Observations on: "Principles of Training" section.

OBSERVATIONS ON:

PRINCIPLES OF TRAINING

INTRODUCTION:

Covered within this chapter are a cross section of observations ranging from *Awase* (blending) to *Reigi* (etiquette). The individual observations do not appear in a particular order of significance, for every element of training whether physical, mental, or spiritual carries an equal level of importance. Each heading within this section could most certainly fill a volume of its own. The abridged and hopefully unpretentious observations to be found here are aimed at the stimulation of the reader's further personal exploration. Immersion in training on an intellectual as well as physical plane is necessary if one is to begin to perceive the powerful development of the spirit inherent in the honest rigorous endeavor of *Aikido*. Each and every element involved in training is an integral part of the overall picture; no one element should be overlooked or practiced with a lackadaisical attitude. Commanding the presence of mind to remain vigilant to the slightest of details leads to a clearer comprehension and greater ability to respond effectively and deal decisively with even the most complex of situations. The saying, "There are no grand *Satori* (enlightenment)," should serve to emphasize the necessity of understanding the essential nature of the principles of training. Therefore, this section will approach a number of training principles from the point of explaining the intrinsic nature of their given names. It is the responsibility of each *Aiki-Deshi* (student of *Aikido*) to take this kernel of knowledge and, through unfeigned resolve, seek to expand upon it a thousand fold. It is important to remember that no description can ever fully convey nor do complete justice to a person, place, event, or idea; refraining from excessive intellectualizing, one should seek to understand through arduous training.

KEIKO

Commonly referring to practice or training, *Keiko* can be more accurately translated as "reflecting on times past." It becomes clear from this translation that *Keiko* should convey a much deeper meaning for those involved in *Aikido*. Although accurate as a general reference to training, *Keiko* should only be used if the training consists of the underlying principles implied by the term *Keiko*, otherwise the Japanese word *Renshu* (lit. practice/drill) would prove a more accurate label. In addition to the physical application, *Keiko* brings a state of mental endeavor to daily training, asking that we explore by means of countless duplication the techniques and their ethics of practice as laid down through great effort by *O'Sensei*. *Aikido Keiko* demands that we bring an open selflessness to our practice, allowing for learning not only from the distant past but also from each elapsed moment as well. The term *Keiko*, which first appeared in written form in the *Kojiki* (records of ancient matters, circa 712 A.D.), is valid only if approached from a point of understanding and consideration for the past and those that have gone before, and a deep commitment to training on all levels of mind, body and spirit. Each time the *Aiki-Deshi* (student of *Aikido*) dons the *Dogi* (way-uniform/training attire), the challenge of the future of *Aikido* can be met, and the potential of *O'Sensei's* way of *Aiki* can become a reality through "reflecting on times past."

DOJO

Translated as "way place" or "training hall of the way," the term *Dojo* is found among many of the training methods of Japan, not excluding those of religions such as *Shinto* and Buddhism. To interpret *Dojo* only as a reference to the actual building in which training is conducted would lead to a great injustice, serving to weaken and dilute the depth of consciousness attainable through the diligent endeavor required in *Aikido*. To illustrate this point, a comparison has been made of two terms often used in martial arts. First, we have the term studio. It is my observation that the primary focus of the studio is directed toward the growth of the owner/instructor's bank account. Second, we have the term school, which seems to be targeted at stroking the ego of the instructor as well as his wallet. In contrast, within the traditional *Dojo*, the emphasis is placed on the continuation and propagation of the art itself. When one allows for no opening or compromise within his application of this principle during training, the focus of striving for knowledge is shifted away from the self, yet the means for self-development not only remains but also becomes powerfully magnified. Therefore, knowledge is seeded internally and allowed to grow pure to its nature, unaffected by an over abundance of perceived personal desire. This is also one of the many manifestations of *Masakatsu Agatsu* (correct victory, self victory). The definition "way place" asks that we become earnestly engrossed within our surroundings as a vital part of training.

KAMIZA-SHOMEN

The term *Kamiza* is used to represent the "upper seat" of the *Dojo* (training hall). We can better understand the importance placed on the *Dojo Kamiza* when we look at the literal translation of the two-word composition. Translated as "deity," the word *Kami* should not be taken to mean God in the Judeo-Christian sense, but rather as a deity inherent in the awareness of nature as in ancient *Shinto*. The word *Za* translated means "seat" as in *Shoza* or "front seat," the area at the front of the mat reserved for the *Sensei* (instructor). The *Dojo*

Kamiza is not, nor should it ever be made a place of worship. The *Kamiza* is the point within the *Dojo* that the honor, respect, and appreciation for the Art, the Founder, and those dedicated to the *Do* (way) past, present, and future, is focused. The *Kamiza* is a place to concentrate and bring the *Deshi* to center, before and after engaging in the rigorous and often precarious endeavors of training. Within the *Dojo* the portion of the mat designated as the front is called the *Shomen* or "front/head of the mat." Most traditional *Aikido Dojo* place within the center of the *Shomen* some form of *Tokonoma* or "alcove." Within the upper left hand section of the *Tokonoma* is placed a picture of *O'Sensei Ueshiba Morihei*, Founder of *Aikido*. It is the job of the *Sempai-Deshi* (senior students) to keep the *Shomen*, *Tokonoma*, and *Kamiza* spotlessly clean, and to see that they are at no time misused. The *Kamiza* is the seat of integrity of the *Dojo*; if it is not valued by a *Deshi*, the loss of respect will ultimately be of the self. The *Kamiza* is a living part of the significant differences separating the traditional *Aikido Dojo* from the common gymnasium.

SENSEI

Though most commonly interpreted as "teacher," the term *Sensei* can be more literally translated as "one who has gone before." Keeping this literal translation in mind, it seems obvious that we would wish to learn from a teacher who has had personal experience and could guide us by the hand painlessly past the pitfalls of training. But conversely, the most significant function of *Sensei* may be the ability to lead the *Deshi* (students) to the threshold of seemingly impassable obstacles, give them the raw materials, and then wait patiently on the other side. Having said this, it is easy to see that it is not *Sensei's* role to be the *Deshi's* friend. A friend could not ask that you face your worst enemy, namely the self, each time you step into the *Dojo* (training hall). In the *Dojo* the word of *Sensei* is law. If the *Deshi* steps onto the mat with an ear to the self, he or she will be smothered by the self, therefore the teaching of the *Sensei* becomes not only the object of learning but also the means by which to detach and do battle with the self. The *Sensei* must embody the essence of *Shoshin* and should possess the qualities of a living example of the modern day *Shugyosha* (see respective sections). When compared to the title of *O'Sensei* (great teacher/one who has gone a great distant before), respectfully given to *Aikido* Founder *Ueshiba Morihei*, we cannot but wonder of the untold difficulties one must face to fill even the shoes of the typical *Sensei*. The *Sensei* must constantly inwardly police both thought and action, often setting aside or even abandoning personal desires for the sake of the art. An admirable *Sensei* deserves respect, trust, honesty, and deep caring, but never should the *Deshi* give, nor the *Sensei* seek worship. It should be noted that in recent years the proliferation of unqualified (this word is used for the lack of a better/stronger one) individuals instructing martial arts has become alarming. It is the difficult but necessary task of the novice to be completely open to both the character of the *Dojo* and spirit of the instructor and students before committing himself to training.

SEMPAI-KOHAI

Sempai-Kohai separately translated denote "senior" and "junior" and are the terms used to identify the *Deshi's* (student's) seniority or lack thereof within the *Dojo* (training hall). Although *Sempai* is a title which may be used to address a senior, *Kohai* should never be used in this manner. *Kohai* is a term used most often when referring to a group of students at a given level. The terms *Yudansha* (of *Dan* rank, black belt level) and *Mudansha* (below *Dan* rank) convey to the novice the most distinguishable separation of rank, but it is the sometimes awkward *Sempai-Kohai* relationship which is the most significant. Though to a *Kohai* anyone who has priorly initiated training and continued in an uninterrupted manner should be considered *Sempai*, the term is most often used in addressing a senior *Yudansha* other than the instructor. Just as the *Kohai* is responsible for always acting in a respectful manner to the *Sempai*, it is equally or even more important that the *Sempai* remain diligently aware of their responsibility toward the *Kohai*. Among the many duties such as the safety and moral support of the *Kohai*, the *Sempai* must always demonstrate, by example, the proper path for continued development under the direction of their *Sensei* (instructor). Even among the most senior *Aikido Sensei* there exists an understanding of who is whose *Sempai*. With such an impressive example as given by these esteemed *Sensei*, it seems clearly evident that the *Deshi* must never overlook the positive humbling nature which the *Sempai-Kohai* method brings to training.

REIGI

Reigi, translated as "etiquette," is the term used when referring to the observance of essential protocol within the *Dojo* (training hall). The basis for the *Aiki-Deshi's* (student) adherence to *Reigi* within the *Dojo* (training hall) stems from the necessity of invoking and maintaining an atmosphere and platform for safe yet rigorous training. Mistakenly, *Reigi* is often thought of as merely the formality of the bow, but this should not be the case, for *Reigi* can be a vehicle to personal control over behavior in all affairs. Adherence to the practice of *Reigi* requires that we not only control the movement of the body but also tether the reins of our ambiguous mind. Though notably different from one *Ryu* (style/school) to another, the benefit of *Reigi* comes from its utilization as an internal and personal form of development. Whether they are familiar with the term or not, the attainment of a deep and intimate understanding of *Reigi* is an unfailing quality which may be found in all exceptional individuals. To develop on the path of *Aiki* we must actively take a position which encourages a deep commitment to honesty and right action, both in ourselves and, by example, in those around us. The foundation and essential attributes needed to develop *Reigi* are found within the correct practice of *Aikido*, but from within the individual must come the level of commitment necessary to comprehend life's connection to the vital and ever-present function of *Reigi*.

BUDO

Looking closely, we find the term *Budo* to be a composite of two words, *Bu* (martial) and *Do* (way). Often the term "martial arts" is offered as a translation of *Budo*, but this is an improper definition and one which more closely defines the Japanese term *Bujutsu* (martial art/science) i.e. martial principles set forth for the sake of war. Therefore the term "martial way" is one which defines *Budo* as martial principles applied to personal/spiritual development for the betterment of mankind and his environment, i.e. productive not destructive in nature. This may at first seem a difficult paradox to understand when faced with the fact that *Aikido* is such a dynamic art, until we remember that *O'Sensei* firmly believed *Aikido* to be an art of loving protection for all things. Though other arts come under the category of *Budo*, we as *Aiki-Deshi* (students of *Aikido*) should keep the founder's beliefs and desires for his art foremost in our thoughts during practice as well as in our representation of the "martial way" of *Aikido* in daily life.

AIKI

The word *Aikido* has as its main component the term *Aiki*, which can be traced to a supplemental level of use within a number of the older martial arts of Japan. When applied to the art developed by *O'Sensei*, *Aiki* maintains its older attributes while at the same time expanding upon them greatly. Separating the two-term composition, *Ai* can be best translated as "harmony or union," while *Ki* depicts "energy/life-force/spirit." *Aiki* therefore takes on the meaning of "spiritual harmony." It should be clearly noted that "spirit" should not be taken in a religious context, but rather denotes the essence which makes each of us a powerful entity, separate from all others and at the same time bound absolutely to all things. In the doctrine of ancient Japanese arts, the term *Aiki* was primarily applied to *Waza* (technique) which embodied the ability to perceive and subsequently nullify an opponent's attack. This concept of perception and nullification is so integral to *Aikido* as to be utilized in the application of all *Waza* within its basis. *Aikido* expands upon this by applying the art of blending, both physically and mentally, not only with an attacker but also with our total environment. With honest rigorous endeavor, *Aiki* becomes a means of overcoming adversity on all levels of existence, bringing under control even the most difficult of adversaries, the self. It is again necessary to make another note here, the *Aiki* of *Aikido* is finding itself explained and utilized more and more as only soft and circular movements. Though the *Aiki* of *O'Sensei* embodies and embraces these movements, it is also an *Aiki* which cuts powerfully to the very heart of the attack, exercising immediate and total control over the adversary/situation. The *Aiki* of *O'Sensei Ueshiba Morihei's Aikido* is a living paradox, a genuinely beautiful violence and a truly peaceful martial way. There is no means by which one can convey the entire significance of *Aiki* by either words or actions. *Aiki* cannot be assimilated as physical technique alone, but instead absorbed as a seed for knowledge which must be painstakingly cultivated. The *Do* (way) of *Aiki* as set forth in *Aikido* by *O'Sensei* is a unique gift which should be cherished and preserved intact for future generations.

KOKYU & KI

In *Aikido* the terms *Kokyu* (breath) and *Ki* (energy/life-force/spirit) are not one and the same, nor does one exist solely because of the other, nor can one exist fully without the other. *Kokyu* is the conduit or channel through which can be expressed the vigorous positive nature of *Ki*. By developing, polishing, and sharpening the edge of our spiritual blade while opening and releasing the compassion trapped deep within our hearts, we may envision the *Ki* of *O'Sensei's Aikido* as an ability to employ the power of all things in nature for the betterment and protection of all things. The literal translation of "breath" for the term *Kokyu* is both correct and incorrect in its applied usage in connection with the practice of *Aikido*. In *Aikido*, embracing the belief that one must inhale fully while entering and exhale powerfully while executing technique, will serve only to disrupt the spontaneous flow of ascertaining and deciphering the essential nature of *Kokyu* found amidst correct training. When we are born we draw our first breath and as we die we draw our last, yet it is the power of the breath we draw during the interim in which our life exists. If we become excited, anxious, or ill, our breath is disturbed; we are aware of it and become distressed. Whereas when we are calm, composed and healthy, our breath flows naturally, is unnoticed and does not distract us. Therefore the power of *Kokyu* and its ability to set forth and act as a channel for *Ki*, comes from being able to breathe freely and undisturbed even in the face of great turmoil. There are infinite denotations of the meaning of the term *Ki*, which may be loosely translated as "energy/life-force/spirit." In Japan, *Ki* is often used to describe things both animate and inanimate, positive and negative. You will by no means find within this text the definitive definition, nor for that matter, did *O'Sensei* leave us with the answers written in stone. Developed through wholehearted endeavor in *Aikido* training, we unearth the latent ability to channel a boundless ocean of positive *Ki*. Wisely, through the efforts of *O'Sensei*, we find that this potential can only be released through the compassion within our hearts. This is the *Ki* with which we are concerned in *Aikido*. It cannot be stated too strongly that growth of the positive nature of *Ki* is the goal of *Aikido*, and that the use of this power should only be applied with the greatest of moral conviction and right action. *Aikido* is *O'Sensei's* way of showing us a power much greater than that of the physical body, yet using the physical body as the means of exploring the positive potential of coming together with nature in mind, body, and spirit.

SEIKA-TANDEN

Alternately referred to as *Hara* or One-Point, the term *Seika-Tanden* may be translated as "central point of the lower abdomen." Pertaining to the area located two to four inches below the navel, *Seika-Tanden* is believed to be both the physical and spiritual seat of the human body. This analogy is not hard to understand when related to the material body, but many persons find this difficult to comprehend when attributed to the spiritual substance of an individual. If we look closely we can find a good number of references within our own western culture in regards to this subject, i.e. "calm down," "get yourself centered," "pure gut instinct" etc. As spoken of previously in this section, the *Aiki-Deshi* must develop a strong base of *Ki*, which is then channeled by the power of *Kokyu*. Amplified by the principles of *Seika-Tanden*, we become aware that the extension of *Ki* by the power of *Kokyu* must emanate from the region of the lower abdomen. When placing the mind, body, and spirit within the *Seika-Tanden*, we are able to unify our thoughts and actions. Powerful, precise, and balanced movements of the body originate from the *Seika-Tanden*. When the potential of the mind is first compressed into the center, not only does the process of thought and action become clearer, but we minimize the often mistaken occurrence of permitting the mouth to lead the body. Developing the principles of *Seika-Tanden* allows for the inherent release of the vital ability and combined efforts of mind, body, and spirit. All definitions of *Seika-Tanden* are esoteric by nature but of utmost importance to the principles of training.

TAKEMUSU-AIKI

"The spontaneous and prolific creation of technique, one upon another in rapid succession, embodied with the principles of *Aiki*," furnished with the rather lengthy preceding translation, it is within reason to state that this communicates only a fraction of the meaning embraced by the expression *Takemusu-Aiki*, as coined by *O'Sensei* (*Ueshiba Morihei*, Founder of *Aikido*). The true *Budo* (martial way) as expressed in the unrestricted form of *Takemusu* exists in the *Aiki* developed within the benevolent heart of the sincere *Deshi* (student), seeded by principle, watered by technique, and cultivated by honest endeavor. By nature, *Takemusu-Aiki* is the foremost expression of *Aikido*. Without exaggeration it is safe to say that, to date, *O'Sensei* has been the only one to have reached this level. It is often misinterpreted that free-form experimentation with technique is the path of *Takemusu*, but this is by no means the proper direction. "Enter with form, exit formless"; using this maxim as an indicator, it should become clear that the proper approach cannot be found in the attempt to rush toward understanding the elevated principles of *Takemusu*, but instead must be slowly manifested through understanding the intrinsic nature of the fundamental principles of *Kihon Waza* (basic technique). To elaborate on this point, I suggest that we take as a model the commitment to training of those such as *Doshu Ueshiba Kisshomaru* (son of the Founder of *Aikido*), whose dedication to the development of precise *Ki-No Nagare* (*Ki*-flow) technique is unmatched, and *Saito Morihiro Sensei*, who is unswayable in his devotion to foundation technique. Only through a level of diligence such as this, may we hope to uncover the correct path to *Takemusu-Aiki*.

DO

The term *Do*, most simply put, translates to mean "way" or "the way you travel the path of your life's training." *Do* and *Michi* (path) are two Japanese terms which are too often mistakenly interchanged. On the one hand, *Michi* is the path which one takes, i.e. the direction of one's life, whereas *Do* is the essence, the taste, the feel, the beginning, the middle, the end, the catalyst for principled growth along the path. Once utterly immersed in the *Do*, it courses through you, bringing about positive development on all levels of the mind, body, and spirit. *Aiki* in itself has existence, but only through becoming absorbed within the *Do* can we even begin to embrace its power and compassionate nature as set forth by *O'Sensei*. Once grasped, the *Do* of *Aikido* can lead to the clear-sighted ability to comprehend and absorb the *Do* within all things, to perceive their *Michi*, and walk with them, not against them, toward the completion of their journey.

KOKORO

Translated as "heart" or "fortitude of the spirit," the term *Kokoro* used in the context of *Aikido* refers to the cultivated perseverance needed to sustain multi-leveled rigorous training. *Aikido* as a *Michi* (path) is not only as steep as a mountain, but also has no reachable top (if you meet someone who claims he has conquered the peak, just step over him and continue on). To face such an endless endeavor one must develop a strong and untainted willpower, for sheer desire cannot survive in the face of such an undertaking. When, through training, we are able to make the transition from the want to learn to learning, from the desire to overcome to overcoming and from the need to succeed to succeeding, we find that the elimination of want/desire/need have been accomplished through the beginnings of the development of *Kokoro*. Bringing about a true "fortitude of the spirit" should be the selfless ambition of all those involved in the art of *Aikido*.

AGATSU

Translated as "self victory" or "victory over the self," the term *Agatsu*, in conjunction with the terms *Masakatsu* (correct victory) and *Katsuhayabi* (moment of swift victory), appears often in the calligraphy left behind by *O'Sensei*. The phrase *Masakatsu-Agatsu-Katsuhayabi* can best be translated as "the moment of correct victory over the self." As a personal observation, I would like to suggest that whether a person's lifetime consists of ten years or a hundred years it is but a wink in the eye of time. The responsibility of all human beings should be one of striving to confront and overcome the weaknesses inherent in the ultimate freedom of self-controlled destiny. It is my strong belief that *O'Sensei* meant for the *Do* (way) of his *Aiki* to be one which may be used toward this purpose. When immersed in correct and rigorous daily training, the core of the training principles of *Agatsu* will become self-evident and of great value to our *Aikido* as well as our personal lives.

SHUGYO

The definition "austere training" which is most commonly used in reference to the term *Shugyo* must not be interpreted solely to denote hard or strenuous training. Instead we should look further into the various elements which comprise the contemporary *Deshi's* (student) level of commitment to *Shugyo* within the practice of *Aikido*. To begin to do this, we must first understand the extent of the commitment of those in the past who have followed the path of the *Shugyosha* (one dedicated to *Shugyo*). It has been said that the olden day *Shugyosha* were men who had given up everything in life for their training. Traveling from town to town and from prefecture to prefecture, the *Shugyosha* survived on pennies a day, often living off of the charity of others. Frequently living a secluded life, the *Shugyosha* were for the most part interested only in self-examination of their art and personal development. A most vivid example of devotion to a slightly more modern approach to *Shugyo* in the late eighteen hundreds and early nineteen hundreds can be found in *O'Sensei Ueshiba Morihei*, Founder of *Aikido*. *O'Sensei* not only placed great stress on his home and family life, turning his every endeavor into *Shugyo*, but ultimately, in an act which would require his full life's work and demand great dedication of those who followed, placed both himself and *Aikido* on the block for public scrutiny. *O'Sensei's* life-long dedication to training body, mind, and spirit on the level of *Shugyo* was instrumental in fostering the development of traditional *Aikido*. Now the question must be asked, "Is *Shugyo* a part of the contemporary martial artist's training?" In the instance of *Aikido* the answer is a resounding yes. Even the average *Deshi*, training in the *Dojo* two or three times a week, not only must subject themselves to the rigors of physical conditioning but also strive to develop a stalwart and positive spirit. This can only happen when the *Deshi* are touched by the essence of the *Aiki* of *O'Sensei* and drawn to apply this *Do* (way) in everyday life, allowing it to direct their lives toward one of implementation, not morose complacency. *Shugyo* may be a large part of the practice of the modern day *Aiki-Deshi*, but only if they never sway from their devotion to life as a great opportunity for *Keiko* (training, see *Keiko*). *Aikido* is truly the art which allows those with dedication and resolve to taste the flavor of positive *Shugyo*.

SHOSHIN

Shoshin or "beginners mind" can be more literally translated as "first mind." To begin to recognize the essential principles of training within *Shoshin*, we must consider carefully the meaning of "first mind." When initially approaching a subject about which we know nothing, we are open to absorbing even the smallest detail. But once, and this is a big once, we begin to realize we have gleaned a smattering of understanding, we have a tendency to cross reference all subsequent knowledge to this perceived understanding, rather than allowing for a natural unhampered flow of learning. Playing one idea off another or even separating them entirely, unreasonably requires that we hold a concept to be undeniably and unyieldingly true. The saying, "When the fruit is growing it is alive, but once ripe it withers," holds tremendous relevance to the subject of *Shoshin*. The stumbling blocks in applying *Shoshin* in daily training are many leveled, not the least of which is the same one we have faced in maintaining the open mindedness, desire, and natural ability to learn that we so effortlessly expressed as children. *Shoshin* is the mind of the learner not the mind of the knowing, for the knowing can never see with the wide-open eyes of the true beginner. It is intriguing to note that upon entering an *Aikido Dojo* (training hall), the new *Deshi* (student) is provided with the gift of the title *Shoshinsha* (a beginner, externally denoting a level below the actual grading system). The *Shoshinsha* then sets out in great earnest to shed the tag of beginner, while hopefully the *Sempai* (seniors) can be found working even more zealously to internally attain its quintessence. It has been said that near to his passing, *O'Sensei* was heard to have remarked, "This old man is a beginner." On the heels of this subtle yet ingeniously cunning declaration, it can only be hoped that each and every *Aiki-Deshi* endeavors to cultivate *Shoshin* and develop the spirit of a timeworn *Shoshinsha*.

IN-YO

The Japanese equivalent of the ancient Chinese principles of Yin-Yang, the terms *In-Yo* are the manifestations of positive-negative, male-female, internal-external, good-bad. *In* represents the negative principles inherent in nature while *Yo* denotes the positive principles. The most readily noticeable usage of the principles of *In-Yo* in the practice of *Aikido* can be seen in the application of *Irimi* (*Omote*) and *Tenkan* (*Ura*) movements in response to an attack. "When the attack is one of *In* respond with *Yo*, when one of *Yo* prevail with *In*." This is a phrase which is not only applicable to *Aikido* but is often associated with a good number of the older *Kenjutsu Ryu* (sword schools). One of the primary difficulties an attacker faces in handling a well applied *Aikido Waza* (technique) stems from the unpremeditated application of the principles of *In-Yo*. "Turn when pushed, enter when pulled" are two sayings heard virtually from the outset of training, but it must be understood that for *In-Yo* principles to be manifested instantaneously as the situation warrants, we must be open to the *In* within the *Yo* and see clearly the *Yo* within the *In*. Being unquestionably and astutely aware of the constant flux of *In-Yo* within the self is one of the embodiments of the state of *Nen* (centered in thought, deed, and moment). If one stops to analyze an attack he or she will be consumed by it. "Perceive not with the eyes but with the body, move not with the body but with the mind, assess not with the mind but with the spirit." This phrase should stand to warn us not to singularly focus on a search for the properties of *In-Yo*, for the principles of *In-Yo* will present themselves freely through the wholehearted practice of the *Aikido* set forth by *O'Sensei*.

<u>KATSUJINKEN</u>

The essence of the definition of the term *Katsujinken*, "the sword that gives life," is located at the very heart of mankind's role in the order of things. "Only within the capacity to devastate can arise true compassion." Ponderous as this statement at first appears, it is nonetheless one which all *Aiki-Deshi* (students of *Aikido*) should strive to understand; for man alone possesses the ultimate power of the human mind, a power which brings with it the cognizant choice of being either destroyer or caretaker. It seems quite pitiful that for the most part man has chosen the path of *Satsujinken*, "the sword that takes life," to that of *Katsujinken*. Since the passing of *O'Sensei*, a disturbing trend has emerged among a number of instructors; in the guise of "peace and love" this trend is misguidedly aimed at the removal of martial principles from the practice of *Aikido Waza* (technique), subsequently creating a watered down and ineffective art. The *Bujutsu* (martial art/science) of the Japanese *Bushi* (warriors) were arts unsurpassed for their strength and effectiveness in dealing with the destruction of an enemy. The genius of the Founder, *O'Sensei Ueshiba Morihei*, was to take these attributes and, while maintaining their potency, transform them into a pure and unique *Budo* (martial way), one with the capacity to face the enemy on all levels, external or internal, while polishing the blade of *Katsujinken* to understand man's true benevolent nature. *Aikido* as set forth by *O'Sensei* is a means through which to build both a powerful body for the martial arts and develop the fortitude necessary to wield the sword that gives, not takes life. *Katsujinken* is by far one of the most important underlining principles of *Aikido*, one which should serve to drive each *Deshi* to train with tremendous determination and an ever-open heart.

IRIMI-TENKAN

Irimi, the act of "entering or entering into," and *Tenkan*, the act of "turning or turning off of," are two terms tantamount to the practice of *Aikido*. Though commonly interchanged with *Omote*, "area to the front," and *Ura*, "area to the rear," when used in the verbal identification of a given technique, the terms *Irimi-Tenkan* are further endowed with the properties of physical as well as directional movement. *Irimi* denotes the act of entering with the body in a manner which slices to the very core of the attack, imploding then exploding the combined energies of the interchange i.e. draining the lake from the center. *Tenkan* indicates the act of turning the body so as to circularly lead and redirect *Uke's* negative force, while combining it with the intensity of *Nage's* movement to create controllable positive energy i.e. draining the lake by rechanneling its waters. Within the pages of this book the terms *Irimi-Omote* and *Tenkan-Ura* have been placed in parentheses at the side of *Waza* (technique), reflecting their interchangeability from *Dojo* to *Dojo* (training halls). It is hoped that by doing so there will ensue a feeling for the flavor as well as the execution of the *Waza*. It should be noted that placing such an incomplete definition on *Irimi-Tenkan* is somewhat of a disservice, for the full meaning can only be realized at the instant of execution. Through painstakingly investigating the properties of *Irimi-Tenkan* expressed in the movements of *Kihon Waza* (basic technique), the awareness of why they are so entrenched within the very nature of *Aikido* will become strikingly evident.

AWASE

The primary component of the phrase *Ken-No Awase* (a form of paired sword training), the term *Awase* alone can be translated as "blending." The movements and moral application of *Aikido Waza* (technique) are based on the physical blending of one's body with that of the attacker while simultaneously bending or dissuading the mental attitude of the attacker from its aggressive direction via the employment of unsettling and often painful technique. Therefore, *Awase* is not only blending your body correctly with that of the attack, but it is also the act of reading and moving harmoniously to negate the negative nature of the psychological intent of the attacker. *Awase* begins even before the first breath of aggression and ends only long after the conflict has been resolved. Once functionally understood through *Kihon Waza* (basic technique), *Awase* becomes the channel for the application of *Ki-No Nagare Waza* (flowing technique, see *Nagare*). Working diligently with *Ken* (sword) in slow yet fully focused paired practice is a powerful way to both develop and reinforce the proper application of *Awase* in *Tai-Jutsu* (body arts). It should be pointed out that training to attain an understanding of *Awase* should not be restricted to *Waza* alone. Applying your attention wholeheartedly to such things as *Reigi* (formalized etiquette, see *Reigi*) can form a solid base toward the development of *Awase*. The acquirement and utilization of *Awase* is as crucial to *Aikido* as is breath to the human body.

MUSUBI

Translated as "knot," the term *Musubi* is most often heard in the phrase *Ki-No Musubi* or "the tying of *Ki*." If we look at the essence of the word "knot" we find within our mind an image of two pieces of rope tied together, so that if one end is pulled the other responds equally. Expanding on this analogy, the *Aiki-Deshi* (student of *Aikido*) is asked to take this basic concept and learn to respond to even the slightest intent, thought, or action of the attacker, to breathe in his mental as well as physical posture, and be ready to explode with the appropriate *Waza* (technique) into each *Suki* (opening) at the instant it is presented. *Musubi* demands that we tie ourselves to the intent of the attacker long before the moment of physical contact and remain linked in spirit even after the encounter has ended. Here we find *Zanshin* or "lingering spirit" as the term most often used to describe the non-physical bond which must survive beyond the proper execution of *Waza*. The philosophy embraced by *Musubi* may be employed not only in aggressive confrontation but equally in every aspect of life, i.e. to be knotted to each moment; to be linked fully with our surroundings; to discern truth from fiction, right from wrong, good from bad, when to respond and when action is not necessary. This is a small fraction of the meaning of *Musubi*, which is a large principle in the training of *Aikido*.

NAGARE

Literally translated as "flow," the term *Nagare*, heard most often in the phrase *Ki-No Nagare*, refers to the "flow of *Ki* (energy)" inherent in all things. In *Aikido*, *Ki-No Nagare* indicates the act of blending, redirecting, and increasing or decreasing the energies brought about by *Nage* (defender/thrower) initially engaging *Uke* (attacker/receiver) in a dynamic rather than static manner. When the rays of the sun pass over a rock, the rock absorbs and then dispels the sun's heat naturally. When a strong wind presses against a willow branch, it bends gracefully until the wind has subsided. When you step on the business end of a rake, it most likely will snap up and strike you in the forehead. These three examples hold the essence of *Nagare*. The rock is given animation by the heat; only the weakness of relying on our eyes holds us from this knowledge. The willow hides from us a great hidden stillness, but only because our mind cannot be drawn from the chill of the passing wind. And finally, it is only our desire to stride boldly forward, which leaves us open to becoming a wide-eyed victim of the rake. To move with the intent of *Uke* while not being drawn in by your surroundings or mesmerized by your inner voice and preconceived notions, is only the beginning of the depth of awareness which the practice of *Aikido Waza* (technique) in *Ki-No Nagare* form holds in store. But a word of caution should be noted, for *Ki-No Nagare* must come as a natural progression in the art of *Aikido* and cannot be pushed or forced ahead of a thorough and in-depth understanding of all aspects of *Kihon Geiko* (foundation training). If you become bored with the basics, think of the animation within the rock, if you are excited by the dynamic movements of the *Sempai* (seniors), think of the stillness of the willow, and if that does not help, look out for the rake.

ATEMI

Defined as "strike," the term *Atemi* contains dual purpose for the *Aiki-Deshi* (student of *Aikido*). While arts such as *Karate* are primarily based on *Ate Waza* (striking technique), *Aikido* finds its foundation in *Nage-Katame Waza* (throwing/immobilizing technique), supplemented only periodically by the use of *Atemi*. The majority of *Atemi* in *Aikido* are directed toward *Suki* (openings) in vital points of the body for the primary purpose of distracting and unbalancing the attacker. The secondary purpose can be found on the other end of the spectrum, wherein *Atemi* may be utilized as a finalizing blow in the termination of the entrapped attacker. This secondary purpose may be difficult to comprehend in the context of *Aikido*, until we consider that the predecessors of *Aikido* evolved from a background imbued with the arts of *Shinken* (live sword) and *Yari* (spear), which often culminated in the dispatching of the adversary. Today, in most *Aikido Dojo* (training hall), the finalizing applications of *Atemi* are no longer taught, and rightfully so, in light of our present social structure. However, it is disturbing to note that too often the proper usage of distracting/unbalancing applications of *Atemi* are also being overlooked. This form of *Atemi* must not be ignored for it is of vital importance to an integrated understanding of *Aikido*. Utilized at the wrong time or the incorrect manner, *Atemi* can be a hindrance in the application of technique, but when employed properly, *Atemi* endures as an authentic and durable principle in *Aikido* training.

KIAI

To produce anything close to a proper translation of *Kiai*, we must first look at the two components which comprise the word. The term *Ki* may be roughly translated as "energy/life-force/spirit" and is the central character in the structure of the word *Aikido*. The term *Ai* translates as "harmony or union" and is the first character to be found in *Aikido*. Together, these two characters placed in the order forming *Aiki* can be translated as "spiritual harmony," causing one to surmise that the reverse placement of these characters, as in *Kiai*, should relay a similar meaning. This is not entirely the case since *Kiai* brings with it the added dimension of the vocalization of focused energy as it is applied to a given task. Keeping this in mind, the closest definition to the term *Kiai* would be "the shout of *Ki* rushing forth." Used in many of the Japanese arts, *Kiai* is not unique to *Aikido*. Unfortunately, in many *Aikido Dojo*, the practice of employing *Kiai* seems almost foreign. This is particularly disturbing when reminded that *O'Sensei* was said to have had a booming, piercing *Kiai* which he engaged freely during training. *Kiai* as utilized in *Aikido* is the intonation of the accumulated rhythm of the energy of mind, body, spirit, and the *Ki* that binds them. Allowed to gush forth naturally, *Kiai* enhances understanding and employment of the flow of energy involved in the dynamic movements of *Aikido Waza* (technique). *Kiai* should not be forced, but of course must at first be practiced with conscious effort. If you are already a serious *Aiki-Deshi* (student of *Aikido*) but have not experienced the utilization of *Kiai*, it is recommended that you first concentrate on its development during training with *Ken* and *Jo* (sword and staff) and allow for its natural transition into your *Tai-Jutsu* (body arts). For *Kiai* to achieve its position as one of the spirited principles of training, it must become a familiar part of our daily endeavor.

METHODS OF TRAINING

AIKI-SHISEI

(POSTURES OF AIKIDO)

Beginning with *Seiza* (formal seated posture) and followed in the progressive order of *Rei* (formal bow), *Za-Rei* (seated bow), *Ritsu-Rei* (standing bow), *Kamae* (beginning stance), and *Maai* (proper distance) the opening chapter of the "Methods of Training" examines the basic postures found in the practice of *Aikido*. Development of a deep understanding of the facets of integrity and humility as well as physical and spiritual preparedness is to be found in the calmness at the center of *Aiki-Shisei*.

NOTE: Due to space limitations, *Jumbi Taiso* (preparatory exercises) are not covered within this text. A regiment of medium to medium/heavy stretching should be utilized prior to each training session, giving close attention to the ankles, hamstrings, and hips (lower body) and the wrists, shoulders, neck, and erector muscles (upper body).

$SEIZA$ _FORMAL SEATED POSTURE_

1

SEIZA: The formal seated posture used in _Aikido_ is created by forming a triangle consisting of two points in front with knees separated by a minimum distance of two fists (photo #1, front view), and one point in rear with feet held together and big toes crossed, left over right (photo #3, back view). Hands are placed on thighs with fingers pointing slightly inward. Back is held straight with abdomen pressed forward (photo #2, side view).

2

OBSERVATION: _Seiza_ is the receptive mind of the empty cup. It is the posture which allows you to absorb information from your surroundings; whether as in days past, the necessity to respond instinctively to a threat to a lord which you guard, or as in its modern application of being a physical and mental posture allowing one to absorb even the smallest detail during instruction. Once attained, your focus should extend outward to the _Waza_ being demonstrated etc., not inward to discomfort, pain, or personal thoughts.

NOTE: _Seiza_ should be held at all times during formal instruction.

3

REI *FORMAL BOW*

ZA-REI (seated bow): Utilized at the beginning of each class as the formal opening and at the end of class as the formal closing, *Za-Rei* is performed while in the seated posture of *Seiza*.

1

2

3

4

5

From *Seiza* (photo #1), keep back straight, incline upper body forward to 45 degrees while placing both hands simultaneously on mat with thumbs and forefingers forming a triangle (photo #2). Bring head down while keeping elbows to the outside of knees, bow forward (photo #3), holding bow for a three count, or just longer than the instructor (beginning and end of class). Bow is concluded by reversing above sequence (photos #4 #5).

NOTE: It is important to keep buttocks in contact with heels throughout bow.

CONTINUED ☞

ZA-REI *SEATED BOW - SIDE VIEW*

NOTE: A formal seated bow is also used just following the change of each technique during class, or whenever bowed to from *Sciza* by one of equal or higher rank; in the latter, holding bow just longer than that of partner.

OBSERVATION: It is possible to discern one's ability, character, and nature from the performance of his/her *Rei*, such as purposeful, sincere and forthright, or regrettably all too often, sloppy, nonchalant, and arrogant.

RITSU-REI STANDING BOW

RITSU-REI (standing bow): *Ritsu-Rei* is performed toward the *Kamiza* upon entering and exiting the *Dojo* and upon entering and exiting the mat. *Ritsu-Rei* is also performed by facing your training partner at the beginning and end of each set of techniques. When bowed to by one of higher rank, bow must be performed slightly deeper and held just longer than that of your *Sempai* (senior).

Stand in neutral stance with hands at side, heels almost touching, and feet at a 45 degree angle outward from heels (photos #1 #1a, front & side view). With back kept straight, bow forward to a 45 degree angle keeping hands at sides (photos #2 #2a, front & side view). Hold and return to upright position.

NOTE: *Rei* in *Aikido* is a show of respect; whether for *O'Sensei*, your *Sensei*, or your partner, it is ultimately a demonstration of respect for yourself and a mirror of your development. *Rei* in *Aikido* is by no means a religious act, nor should it be treated as one. *Rei* when done correctly is a means of centering and bringing under control the self. Lack of clarity of mind and dedicated purpose is one of the biggest drawbacks to the perfection of *Rei*.

KAMAE *BEGINNING STANCE*

KAMAE (beginning stance): Based on the triangular foot placement of *Hanmi* (T-shaped stance with back foot at 90 degrees), *Kamae* is the embodiment of the state of *Sen-No-Sen* (seizing the initiative). Though outwardly sedate and relaxed in appearance the heart of *Kamae* must be one of instantaneous action.

1

1a

GEDAN NO KAMAE : Low stance (hands)

From posture of *Hanmi*, separate feet by the distance of one natural step, then add one-half foot length to acquire solid foundation. Disposition of weight should be sixty/forty front to rear. Front hip is turned slightly inward with hips thrust forward. Hands are held relaxed and ready at sides (photos #1 #1a, front & side view).

2

2a

CHUDAN NO KAMAE : Middle stance (hands)

A slightly more aggressive posture than *Gedan*, *Chudan* is acquired by adding the forward extension of the hands at center level (photos #2 #2a, front & side view).

OBSERVATION: A strong mental image to enhance your understanding of *Kamae* is that of your lower body drawing energy up from the earth to your center (lower abdominal region) and then out from your center through your upper body.

46

MAAI *PROPER DISTANCE*

MAAI (proper distance): Taken from the words *Ai* (harmony) and *Ma* or *Mae* (before or front), *Maai* can then be translated as "the harmony before action." To achieve this harmony *Nage* must start from a base at which it is necessary for the *Uke* to advance to attempt to invade *Nage's* sphere of energy.

Basic *Maai* is formed by creating a distance from *Kamae* which places *Uke* and *Nage* just out of reach of each other when extending same arm as forward most foot (photo #1). Whenever a weapon is involved, the distance is increased by the length of the weapon, i.e. one weapon, two weapons, etc. (photo #2).

NOTE: *Maai* is not the distance which separates, it is the distance which connects.

OBSERVATION: Remove from your mind the idea that *Maai* is the lull before the storm. Actually *Maai* is the point at which you enter the eye of the hurricane so to speak, for it is important that you have already made a spiritual link with your partner and that the link is held throughout training with that partner, whether *Uke* or *Nage*.

TAI-NO HENKO
(BODY CHANGING)
KOKYU RYOKU TAISO
(BREATH POWER - EXERCISE)

The first three pages of this section deal with *Tai-No Henko* from both side and front views with a number of notations which deserve close attention. Translated as body changing, *Tai-No Henko* refers to the basic blending utilized in both *Irimi* and *Tenkan* movements, and in its *Kihon* (basic, static) form should be made a vital part of daily training. Performing *Tai-No Henko* over and over thousands of times, we come to understand and develop the ability to grasp and control *Uke's* center through the engagement of powerful hip movement. The second segment is comprised of the *Kokyu Ryoku Taiso*. Development of a strong and centered *Seika-Tanden* (*Hara* or one-point) as the center for emanation of energy throughout and beyond our physical body's perceived limitations, is essential to the proper execution of technique within the framework of *Aikido* practice. *Kokyu-Dosa* and *Kokyu-Ho* are the two main *Kokyu Ryoku Taiso* which, in exercise form, teach us the fundamentals of this most difficult task, but very possibly their most important usage is to bring us back to this understanding when we stray during daily *Keiko* (training). Accordingly, *Kokyu Ryoku Taiso* should be given close and thorough study at all levels and from all points of the spectrum, thus giving it its proper place within our lifelong study of *Aikido*.

TAI-NO HENKO *SIDE VIEW*

1

Uke utilizes straight hand grab from *Gyaku-Hanmi* (photo #1).

NOTE: *Uke* must use very strong grip, sending energy through whole arm, and keep this grip even if *Nage* is able to move, i.e. allowing as little air space between gripping palm and held wrist as possible.

APPLIED PRINCIPLES: Gliding forward to align left foot with *Uke*, *Nage* maintains hand alignment with center while drawing in and obliquing hips (photo #2).

NOTE: *Nage* must work to keep shoulders, body weight, and mind down, not allowing them to raise up and produce a postural imbalance.

2

3

Shifting hips to engage *Uke* fully, *Nage* pivots hips to align with *Uke's* direction (photo #3). Maintaining left foot as the axis, *Nage* sweeps right foot back 180 degrees, completing movement in *Gyaku-Hanmi* at *Uke's* side (photo #4). See notation in *Tai-No Henko* front view.

NOTE: *Uke* must remain aware and attuned to *Nage's* movements, always prepared for *Atemi* or application of *Waza*.

OBSERVATION: When a *Yudansha* returns to a beginners class (*Kihon Geiko*), it's not to learn the secrets of *Aikido* - or is it?

4

TAI-NO HENKO

1

The photograph and number sequence of *Tai-No Henko* (front view) correspond with those of the side view presented on the previous page.

2

3

4

4a

INCORRECT

NOTE: Held hand must stay aligned with *Nage's* hips (photo #4) and not be allowed to be drawn into line with *Uke's* center (photo #4a). Holding free hand out equal to that of held hand, allows checking of posture to ensure proper engagement of hips (photos #3 #4), a vital point in all *Waza*.

INCORRECT

INCORRECT

PUSHING - Entering too deeply causes loss of proper shoulder to hip relationship.

PULLING - Turning too shallow causes arm to drag behind and disconnect from hips.

CORRECT

TURNING - Entering obliquely with whole body movement emanating from hips creates powerful link with *Uke*.

NOTE: The inclusion of *Tai-No Henko* in daily training should not be taken lightly. When engaged in the practice of *Tai-No Henko*, we must keep in mind that it is practice not competition, and when faced with a roadblock, we must identify and remedy the problem, not just gun our engine and muscle through.

POST NOTE: *Tai-No Henko* may also be practiced in a *Ki-No Nagare* (*Ki* flow) form, i.e. *Nage* moves just as *Uke* commits to attack, blending in a dynamic rather than static manner. At *Agatsu Dojo* we utilize four sets consisting of twenty-seven paired *Aiki-Taiso*. Regardless of the amount of *Taiso*, it is important to remember static *Tai-No Henko* is the base from which to work.

KOKYU-DOSA: KOKYU RYOKU TAISO

1

2

3

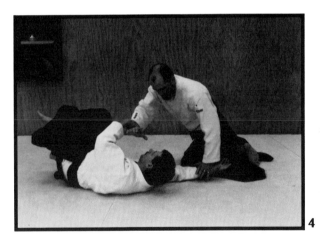

4

5

The first of the two main *Kokyu Ryoku Taiso* begins from a *Ryotetori* hold with both *Uke* and *Nage* in *Seiza* position. Grasped firmly by *Uke*, *Nage* raises both arms toward *Uke* being sure to keep elbows in a low position (photos #1 #2). As *Uke's* balance is broken to the rear, *Nage* cuts left hand over *Uke's* right wrist while rotating torso in and forward, directing *Uke's* balance to side (photos #3 #4). Drawing right knee around to *Uke's* side, *Nage* positions right hand above shoulder, keeping left hand above wrist (photo #5). At this point *Uke* attempts to sit straight up into *Nage's* posture. *Nage's* extension should be sufficient to hold *Uke* without the necessity of pushing down.

NOTE: Both *Kokyu-Dosa* and *Kokyu-Ho* (next page) are means through which one develops the unity of Body, Mind, and Spirit. This bringing together of these essential elements in *Aikido* is the first step toward harmonious interaction not only with *Uke* but also with the world around us. *Aikido* exists to bring down that which is against nature. To begin this process, we must first acknowledge and then bring into accord the elements of Body, Mind, and Spirit. *Kokyu Ryoku Taiso* can play the part of our mirror in this endeavor.

KOKYU-HO: KOKYU RYOKU TAISO

1

NOTE: *Uke* applies strong grip, placing outside hand high.

2

The second of the two main *Kokyu Ryoku Taiso* begins with a *Ryotemochi* (*Morote-Tori*) hold from *Gyaku-Hanmi*. Advancing with left foot forward, *Uke* takes a two hands on one wrist hold while making sure not to be square to *Nage's* free hand (photo #1).

3

Entering deeply to the outside while pivoting hips to align with *Uke*, *Nage* simultaneously rotates held hand counterclockwise while dropping hips below the level of *Uke's* hips. *Nage's* elbow must be held toward *Uke* with shoulder down and tight to *Uke's* shoulder (photo #2).

4

Beginning to rotate hips toward *Uke*, *Nage* slides right foot beneath *Uke's* center. Making sure elbow comes up *Uke's* center line, *Nage* begins to rotate hands to a palms up position while extending held arm across *Uke* (photo #3). *Nage* completes *Kokyu-Ho* by continuing to rotate hips until center is aligned with forward leg and hands are held over *Uke* (photos #4 #5).

5

NOTE: *Nage's* hips are screwed into ground (descending spiral) as arms rise (ascending spiral), head should not follow *Uke* and shoulders must remain down.

OBSERVATION: Just as a flower's roots reach deep into the earth to drink the spring rain and then open their buds with an explosion of beauty reaching for the sky, so should we remember to rotate our hips downward while exploding upward with the power of *Kokyu*.

SABAKI TAISO

(BODY TURNING - EXERCISE)

Introduced within this section are basic examples of both *Tai-Sabaki* (evasive body turning) and *Ken No Tai-Sabaki* (evasive body turning with sword). *Tai-Sabaki* is based on the principle of entering at the proper angle to take full advantage of the *Suki* (dead spot/opening) presented by *Uke's* attack or defense. Developed from aspects of *Shinken* (live sword) and *Yari* (spear), arts which call for entering without receiving a reciprocal blow, *Tai-Sabaki* is the first line of physical action taken by *Nage* in the performance of *Waza* (technique). Performed from the beginning posture of *Hanmi*, *Tai-Sabaki* vividly demonstrates the necessity for the development of powerful yet calm, fluid, responsive hip movement.

1

2

Tai-Sabaki translates as body turning motions. Within the context of *Aikido*, its primary usage refers to the act of evasive postural shifting at the point of initial entry during the execution of *Waza* (technique).

It is important to remember that the *Riai* (arts which collectively constitute a particular style) within *Aikido* is comprised of *Ken* (sword), *Jo* (staff), and *Tai-Jutsu* (body arts/sciences). During *Tai-Sabaki Taiso*, we receive our first small glimpse into the truly combined nature of *Aikido's Riai*, in that one truly expresses the other, i.e. *Tai-Jutsu* arts may be applied as *Jo* arts, etc.

During practice, partners should keep in mind that they are performing *Taiso* not *Waza* (exercise not technique). Utilizing proper *Maai*, each *Taiso* should begin from a calm static base. *Uke* must remember a strong focused attack sets the groundwork for *Nage* to explore the action-reaction and/or reaction-action scenario of *Tai-Sabaki*.

At the point of completion, *Nage* leads disengagement. This is a basic principle of *Ken* and *Jo* practice which should be employed in *Tai-Sabaki*.

3

Starting from *Ai-Hanmi*, *Uke* advances with left *Chudan Tsuki*. *Nage* glides forward and slightly outside, aligning right forearm with *Uke's* left elbow. Throwing back left foot, *Nage* acquires control of center line (see photo at right).

3a

CONTINUED

1

2

3

Starting from *Ai-Hanmi*, *Uke* advances with right *Shomenuchi*. *Nage* glides to outside obliquing hips and applying *Atemi* to *Uke's* temple.

Starting from *Ai-Hanmi*, *Uke* advances with right *Chudan Tsuki*. *Nage* glides to outside engaging both hips and applies *Atemi* to face and ribs simultaneously.

1

2

3

TAI-SABAKI

1

2

3

Starting from *Ai-Hanmi*, *Uke* advances with right *Shomenuchi*. *Nage* steps deeply into the outside of *Uke's* attack, driving arm upward with *Kokyu* power, unsettling *Uke's* balance while controlling center of original attack line.

Starting from *Ai-Hanmi*, *Nage* initiates movement by driving right *Tegatana* (handblade) toward *Uke's* face. At the instant of *Uke's* block, *Nage* steps forward and to the outside grasping nape of neck. Throwing back right foot, *Nage* acquires control of centerline. See lead page of this section for front view.

1

2

3

KEN NO TAI-SABAKI *EVASIVE BODY TURNING WITH SWORD*

1

Starting from *Ai-Hanmi*, *Uchi* glides in with *Shomen-Giri* (downward cut to head). *Uke* matches *Uchi's* cut while gliding forward and slightly to the inside, obliquing hips and delivering *Shomen* (see front view for body alignment).

Oyo Taiso: *Uke* may cut *Uchi* at wrist or block top of *Ken* by adjusting depth of entry.

2

SPECIAL NOTE: When both partners are wielding *Ken* they are designated *Uke-Ken* (receiving sword) and *Uchi-Ken* (attacking sword); *Uke-Ken* always perseveres.

3

3a

NOTE: Photo #3a (left) shows proper hip engagement and angle of entry to the *Suki* (opening) presented by *Uchi's* attack.

KEN NO TAI-SABAKI

1

Starting from *Ai-Hanmi*, *Uchi* glides in with *Shomen-Giri*. *Uke* glides forward to *Uchi's* right, bringing the *Ken* up under *Uchi's* wrists, stopping *Uchi* at top of his upward swing (see front view for body alignment).

Oyo-Taiso: *Uke* may also advance to *Uchi's* left side or straight forward to control *Uchi* at throat with *Tsuki-Giri* (thrusting cut).

2

3a

3

NOTE: Photo #3a (left) shows proper angle of entry. Special note should be taken as to the placement of *Uke's Ken* on *Uchi's* wrist (depth and area of contact).

Starting in *Ai-Hanmi*, *Uchi* glides in with *Shomen-Giri*. *Uke* rotates hips fully, stepping outside to *Uchi's* right, while executing *Chudan Tsuki* (mid-level thrust). *Uke* must remove right foot from centerline (see front view photo).

NOTE: As with all *Sabaki Taiso* it is important that *Uke's* movements are completed at the same time as *Uchi's*.

NOTE: Photo #3a (left) shows the proper angle of entry and depth of engagement of *Uke's* foremost hip.

OBSERVATION: When an opening presents itself, slip in; when none exists, draw *Uchi's* mind.

UKEMI
(THE ART OF RECEIVING)
SHIKKO
(KNEE WALKING)
KOGEKI
(TERMINOLOGY OF ATTACKS)

The term *Uke* refers to the person who attacks then subsequently receives the *Waza* (technique) from *Nage*. Therefore, *Uke* is the receiver and performs *Ukemi* (the art of receiving) to protect himself or herself from harm. Having said this it must be noted that *Ukemi* is also a means through which *Uke* learns and a catalyst for *Nage's* progression. Not to emphasize the necessity for the development of proper *Ukemi* would be to place a giant roadblock in the path of one's progress. Contained within the first portion of this section are examples of the most basic *Ukemi* necessary in daily practice. The second portion examines *Shikko* (knee walking), the means by which *Nage* and *Uke* can move about freely from the seated position of *Seiza*. The final portion of this section deals with the basic forms of *Kogeki* (attacks) as utilized by *Uke*. Each individual *Aiki-Deshi* (student of *Aikido*) is charged with the responsibility of developing the sensitivity as well as the physical and mental properties necessary to take these fundamentals through their basic form to the level of artful expression.

USHIRO UKEMI *BACK ROLL*

1

2

3

To perform *Ushiro Ukemi*, start by stepping back placing left knee on mat with foot to right side (photos #1 #2).

4

5

Rock back making sure to keep your head to left side (photo #3), continuing backward movement, throw both feet over right shoulder (photos #4 #5). Stretching left leg back, place left knee down on mat (photo #6), conclude roll by moving back into standing position (not shown).

NOTE: When left knee is placed down, head goes toward left shoulder, feet go over right shoulder. When right knee is placed down, head goes toward right shoulder, feet go over left shoulder. *Ukemi* in *Aikido* is performed from hip to opposite shoulder (back roll) or arm to opposite hip (front roll). Therefore, it is important that you align hip and opposite shoulder on the directional line in which you wish to roll. It is imperative that you do not roll up or down the spine.

6

MAE UKEMI *FRONT ROLL*

To perform *Mae Ukemi*, start by taking a large step with right foot while extending right arm forward, *Tegatana* (handblade, little finger side of hand) facing outward with thumb down (photo #1). Stretching body forward, place *Tegatana* on mat with fingers pointing back toward foot, throw left foot up and over back while pushing off powerfully with right foot (photo #2).

Following line upward from point of contact of *Tegatana* across shoulder to opposite hip, tuck left leg in behind right knee (photo #3). Placing right foot down at least eighteen inches from back knee, allow momentum and forward motion to bring you to a one knee up, one knee down position (photo #4). Conclude roll by moving into a standing position (not shown).

MAE UKEMI BREAK FALL

Supported form of *Mae Ukemi* is performed by projecting yourself over your own arm while holding and being held firmly by your partner.

NOTE: It is important that hips follow line of shoulder and not be thrown to the outside.

1

2

3

4

1

2

3

4

Solo version of *Mae Ukemi* practice consists of propelling yourself into the air, then snapping hips forward, causing full rotation of body.

NOTE: Projection must be up and outward, not forward and down.

SHIKKO *KNEE WALKING*

Shikko, the basic means of locomotion utilized in the application of *Hanmi-Handachi* and *Suwari Waza*, begins from the formal seated posture of *Seiza* (photo #1). Draw right knee up and forward while curling toes under. Be sure to keep feet together and beneath body during movement (photo #2). Place right knee down and immediately step forward with left knee, keeping toes curled under throughout motion (photo #3). Place left knee down and step forward with right, etc. (photo #4).

1

2

3

4

NOTE: Striving to keep spine erect while placing emphasis on carrying and maintaining body weight in the lower abdomen will insure the ability to perform rapid yet stable movements. After acquiring the ability to move forward freely, experimentation in shifting and turning to angles of 45, 90, 180, 270, and 360 degrees without loss of centralization or focus of purpose is the next step in developing workable *Shikko*.

KOGEKI *ATTACKS*

MAE TORI: FRONT GRAPPLING ATTACK

The following sequence of photos depicts various basic frontal grappling attacks. Virtually all *Kihon Waza* (basic technique) are first learned from static grappling attacks. Paying close attention to the line of attack, it is essential that *Uke* develop and maintain a heightened state of awareness.

KATATETORI :
Straight hand grab

HANTAI (*Ai-Hanmi Katatetori*) :
Cross hand grab

RYOTEMOCHI (*Morotetori*) :
Two hands on one arm hold

RYOTETORI :
Two hand grab, one on one

KATATORI/MUNADORI :
One lapel/shoulder grab

KATATORI SHOMENUCHI :
One lapel grab with overhead strike

KATATORI TSUKI :
One lapel grab with thrusting strike

RYOKATATORI/MUNADORI :

Two lapel/shoulder grab

GYAKU RYOKATATORI/MUNADORI :

Grabbing opposite lapels

USHIRO TORI : GRAPPLING ATTACK FROM REAR

Aikido Waza consist of defensive actions applicable against all forms of attacks from any direction, including attacks from behind. The next sequence of photos depicts various grappling attacks from the rear. As mentioned in the frontal attacks section, *Kihon Waza* are first taught from a static position. Later, within the natural progression of training, *Ki-No Nagare* applications are introduced. *Ki-No Nagare* or *Ki*-flow *Waza* refers to the application of technique in which *Nage* attempts to tie his or her *Ki* (*Ki-No Musubi*) to that of the *Uke's*, prior to the point of firm contact. To perform *Ki-No Nagare* applications to an *Ushiro Tori* attack, *Uke* begins attack in front of or to right angles of *Nage*. It is important to again note that *Ki-No Nagare* be taken as a natural progression, only after the basics and foundation have been laid and concreted (*Yudansha* level) should *Ki-No Nagare* become part of daily training.

USHIRO RYOTETORI :

Two rear wrist grab

USHIRO RYOTETORI :

Wrists pulled behind back

USHIRO HIJITORI :

Two rear elbow grab

USHIRO RYOKATATORI/MUNADORI :

Two rear lapel/shoulder grab

KOGEKI

USHIRO KUBISHIME :

One wrist grab with one arm strangle hold

USHIRO TORI :

Bear hug from behind

USHIRO TORI :

Both arms through elbows from behind

USHIRO TORI :

Full nelson

ERITORI SHOMENUCHI :

Nape of neck grab with overhead strike

USHIRO TORI :

Head pulled back by hair

UCHI : STRIKING ATTACK

Starting from proper distance (see *Maai* section), *Uke* steps forward closing the distance quickly and performs one of three attacks: overhead, straight forward, or to the side. *Uke* should pay close attention to the engagement of hips in delivering strikes.

Initial striking posture

1

2

SHOMENUCHI :

Stepping forward *Uke* performs overhead strike to *Nage's* forehead (photos #1 #2)

1

2

YOKOMENUCHI :

Stepping forward *Uke* performs strike to side of *Nage's* head at temple (photos #1 #2)

1

2

CHUDAN TSUKI :

Stepping forward *Uke* performs thrusting strike to *Nage's* midsection (photos #1 #2)

1

2

MENUCHI TSUKI :

Stepping forward *Uke* performs thrusting strike to *Nage's* face/head (photos #1 #2)

KATAME WAZA

(TECHNIQUES OF IMMOBILIZATION)

In the application of *Aikido, Katame Waza* denotes the act of rendering an attacker immobile at the culmination of a technique. Developed and refined from *Jujutsu* by *O'Sensei, Katame Waza* allows for the full immobilization of an attacker of greater size and strength with a minimum of effort. Minimum effort-maximum effect, does not mean powerful effort should not be put forth, but instead that effort must yield the desired results. This observation holds true in all application of *Aikido Waza*. The following section examines a number of *Katame* applications as employed in both their *Kihon* (basic) and *Oyo* (varied/applied) *Waza* forms. A thorough study of the human anatomy would surely not go to waste in the endeavor to decipher the essence of *Katame Waza*. During the course of day to day training, the *Aiki-Deshi* will come to a rather expeditious realization that much of this knowledge may be gained through serving as *Uke* (one who receives). The close-ups of the *Katame Waza* found in this section should be frequently referred to during the study of the *Waza* within the nucleus of this book.

KATAME WAZA TECHNIQUES OF IMMOBILIZATION

The Japanese word *Katame* when used within the context of *Aikido*, refers to endings applied to techniques which place *Uke* in a state of immobilization, definitively restricting him or her from continued aggressive action. The *Katame Waza* of *Aikido*, in their basic applied forms, consist of techniques which are non-destructive in nature, holding *Uke* immobile through the use of skeletal, musculo, and neurological manipulation. All *Aikido Waza* fall into one of two categories, either *Katame Waza* or *Nage Waza* (techniques of projection). As you advance through the techniques chosen to be a part of this book, you will note that most *Nage Waza* may also have *Katame Waza* applications. *Katame Waza*, from *Uke's* viewpoint, manifests itself on three levels, restrictive yet non-painful, mildly discomforting, and downright intolerable. Therefore *Nage* should seek to firmly and fully control *Uke* with the least amount of unnecessary pain as possible, keeping in mind the reversed encounter that will follow. When *Uke* has been correctly immobilized, striking of the free hand on the mat (or foot, if both arms are restrained) will signal *Uke's* submission. *Nage* should remain keenly alert for this signal, as *Uke* may be quickly approaching his physical limit. If, as *Nage*, one can train with the mental image of pinning himself, his rate of growth and understanding of *Katame Waza* will be greatly increased.

KIHON: BASIC - Endings most frequently used in daily training.

OYO: VARIED/APPLIED - Advanced endings taught at *Yudansha* level.

KIHON: Arm held straight with energy linked from wrist to elbow. Wrist held slightly above mat.

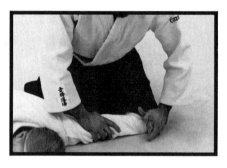

KIHON: Arm held straight, palm turned toward elbow with fingers forward. Energy from back of knuckles to elbow.

KIHON: Extension development. Arm held straight with knees at base of ribs and wrist. Elbow rolled forward by *Tegatana*.

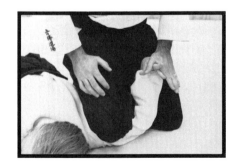

OYO: Arm bent upward with knee on upper arm. Palm down with energy to back of knuckles.

KIHON: Arm bent inward with palm up. Energy directed downward on elbow, toward inner knuckles.

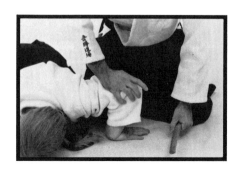

KIHON: Same as previous with *Gokyo* grip (thumb on hand gripping *Uke's* wrist, facing outward). *Tanto Tori* : Relieve *Uke* of knife.

KIHON: Arm held above back with rotation toward head. *Nage* free pins arm to body.

KIHON: Arm held above back with rotation toward head. *Nage* grasps own *Keikogi* (uniform) at shoulder and hip.

KIHON: Arm held above back with palm held upward, rotation toward head. *Nage* free pins with lower arm.

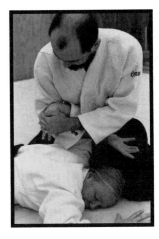

OYO: Same as previous. *Nage* grasps inner wrist.

OYO: Arm held above head with deep incline over body. *Nage* grasps shoulder.

OYO: Same as previous with palm turned up and fingers wrapped downward over *Nage's* elbow.

OYO: Same as previous with palm down and index knuckle rotated toward head. Inner arm low.

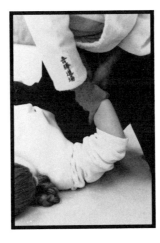

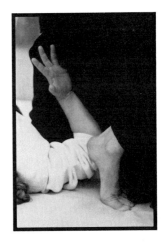

KIHON: Arm bent upward. *Nage* thrusts shin against tricep, applying *Yonkyo* down and to the outside.

KIHON: Arm bent upward. Inner knee in armpit, outer foot forward of elbow. Back of *Uke's* hand against thigh, hip thrust forward applying *Yonkyo*.

OYO: Same as previous. *Nage* pins elbow with heel while thrusting inner hip forward and applies knuckle to spine between shoulder blades.

77

KATAME WAZA

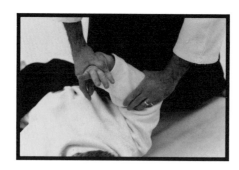

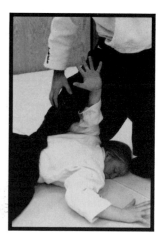

KIHON: Arm straight above back with inner knee against forearm. Energy on back of hand, directed downward toward ear.

OYO: Arm bent above back. Knee thrust forward against wrist while elbow is drawn toward *Nage*.

OYO: Arm held straight above body, free pinned against inner thigh. Outer foot forward of opposite shoulder, hip thrust forward.

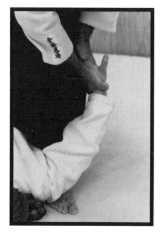

KIHON: Arm bent upward. *Nage* thrusts shin against tricep, applying *Sankyo* down and to the outside.

OYO: Arm bent above back with palm held against outside of inner knee. Knee thrust forward toward back of head.

OYO: Progression of previous. Pinning wrist against back with shin, *Nage* steps forward with outer foot, lifts and draws *Uke's* opposite arm toward center.

KIHON: From *Shiho-Nage*, continuing rotation behind shoulder, *Nage* applies energy through forearm while thrusting hip toward head, arching *Uke's* back.

KIHON: From *Shiho-Nage*, outer hand drives downward on elbow, arching *Uke's* back while inner hand delivers *Atemi*.

OYO: From *Shiho-Nage*, same as previous with hands reversed and *Nage* positioned past *Uke's* head.

78

OYO: From *Sankyo*, hand held low and tight to back, continuing *Sankyo* rotation. Inner knee directly against top of head, outer knee up with hips drawn back.

OYO: From *Kotegaeshi*, stop *Uke* at top center of turnover, pin opposite wrist with foot. Direct energy downward through back of hand and shoulders, to mat.

OYO: From *Ikkyo/Hiji-Kime*, draw opposite arm across waist. Inner foot forward of *Uke's* feet with free pinning focus directed between shoulder blades.

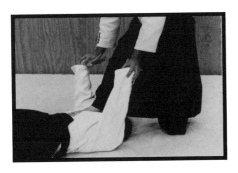

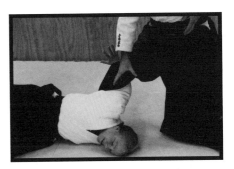

OYO: From *Ryo-Nikyo*, both arms held straight above back with energy applied to back of knuckles, toward head. Heel placed in center of upper back.

OYO: Progression from previous. Slipping right foot into left armpit, *Nage* turns *Uke* onto side, positioning right arm behind knee while drawing hip away from *Uke*.

OBSERVATION: Interaction *Nage / Uke*.

N A G E		**U K E**	
	DO - control self-unrest		DO - relax
	DO - firmly link with *Uke*		DO - breathe normally
	DO - physically, psychologically control *Uke*		DO - exhale at peak of application
	DO - restrain *Uke's* spirit		DO - use as a stretching exercise
	DO NOT - wrestle with *Uke*		DO - remain firmly linked with *Nage*
	DO NOT - become intimidated by *Uke*		DO NOT - disconnect mind from body
	DO NOT - maltreat *Uke*		DO NOT - resist properly executed *Waza*
	DO NOT - give up		DO NOT - act in stupidity

NOTE: It must be clearly understood that *Aikido* is a martial way, and as a martial way it has within its *Waza* the properties of extreme violence. In the instance of *Katame Waza* this takes form as the ability to separate, dislocate, break, or otherwise render completely inoperable any number of *Uke's* body parts. Therefore, one should take great care in the study of *Katame Waza* so that these destructive powers, though understood, will never be used unless justifiably and morally warranted. Otherwise our domination oriented ego-self will severely limit our training to the mere physical realms, causing us to overlook the true essence and uniqueness of *Aikido*. As you develop a deep understanding of the term *Aiki-Musubi*, it will become clear that unnecessary actions are actions which are felt by all.

TAI-JUTSU

(BODY ARTS)

TACHI WAZA

(STANDING TECHNIQUES)

The empty-handed or unarmed applications of techniques within *Aikido* are termed *Tai-Jutsu* (body arts) and make up the bulk of daily training. This section covers *Tachi Waza* (standing techniques). The word *Tachi* has dual meaning, also being used in reference to the *Ken* (sword) as in *Tachi-Dori* (sword taking). Whether engaged in *Taiso* (exercise), *Tai-Jutsu*, *Ken*, or *Jo* (staff) training, it is of utmost importance that the *Aiki-Deshi* (student of *Aikido*) remain fully focused on the task at hand. The heart of *Aikido* is not to be found in casual noncommitted practice; only through honest endeavor of Body, Mind, and Spirit will *Aikido's* essence emerge. Remaining ever attentive to all aspects of training is both the *Aiki-Deshi's* utmost challenge and most powerful tool for development.

IKKYO

(FIRST TEACHING)

Literally translated as "first teaching," *Ikkyo* refers to the first control technique taught in the sequence of *Ikkyo* through *Gokyo*. The challenging usage of *Kokyu-Ryoku* (breath power), *Ki-No Musubi* (tying of *Ki*) and their related principles make the term "first teaching" truly relevant in its relationship to our continued development and growth within *Aikido*. *O'Sensei* has been quoted as having referred to *Irimi-Nage* (entering throw) as the twenty-year technique. This being so, one can only be in awe of *O'Sensei's* insight in not informing his *Deshi* (students) that *Ikkyo* may indeed be the life-long technique, an appropriate reference to the level of endeavor required in this vital basic.

SHOMENUCHI IKKYO *IRIMI/OMOTE*

Uke utilizes overhead strike from *Gyaku-Hanmi* (photo #1).

APPLIED PRINCIPLES: Gliding powerfully forward and to the inside (live side) of *Uke's* attack, *Nage* extends arms upward from center while cutting hips directly through *Uke's* posture. Taking control of *Uke's* elbow from beneath, *Nage* causes *Uke's* weight to shift over *Uke's* back foot (photo #2). Continuing with an instantaneous cut, diagonally down and into *Nage's* center, *Nage* utilizes strong hip rotation to bring *Uke's* arm into a straight position and under control (photo #3).

Thrusting right hip forward, *Nage* steps deeply into *Uke's* posture causing *Uke* to lose balance and place weight on free hand (photo #4). Drawing up back foot, *Nage* pins *Uke* by lowering center firmly to mat (photo #5).

NOTE: *Nage* must never lose the flow of *Kokyu* throughout his body, especially arms. When applying *Ikkyo*, *Nage's* arms and *Uke's* arm should be as one circuit of energy (*Tetsubo*). Alignment of *Nage's* hips should form the base of a triangle, with *Uke's* elbow being the forward most intersecting point.

OBSERVATION: The necessity of fully utilizing basic *Kokyu* principles offers a reasonable explanation for the connotation *Ikkyo* (lit. first teaching), due to its fundamental relationship within all *Waza*.

SHOMENUCHI IKKYO *TENKAN / URA*

Uke utilizes overhead strike from *Gyaku-Hanmi* (photo #1).

APPLIED PRINCIPLES: Stepping powerfully forward, *Nage* aligns left foot with *Uke's* right foot while seizing attacking arm beneath elbow (photo #2).

NOTE: Meeting *Uke's* arm before it builds downward momentum, *Nage* must first control elbow, placing *Uke's* weight on back foot while aligning *Uke's* elbow with original line of his spine (photo #2). Inner arm is power (hand holding elbow), outer arm is direction (hand at wrist).

OBSERVATION: When pinning with *Ikkyo*, *Nage* should keep in mind that the inner hip holds the power to move or drop *Uke* at any time or in any direction. Even though both hips are working in unison just like gears turning, the outer teeth are turning, but it is the inner teeth which are directly applying the combined force.

Throwing back right foot 90 degrees, *Nage* sharply rotates hips clockwise while lowering center firmly to the mat, executing pin (photo #3 #4).

NOTE: *Nage* may pin *Uke* in various degrees within the sphere of *Tenkan*, i.e. 90 degrees (shown), 180 degrees, etc. During the take down, *Nage* pins *Uke's* arm in shoulder-elbow-wrist sequence.

KATATORI IKKYO *IRIMI/OMOTE*

1

Uke utilizes straight hand lapel/shoulder grab from *Gyaku-Hanmi* (photo #1).

APPLIED PRINCIPLES: Moving sharply 90 degrees to right, *Nage* directs *Atemi* (strike) to *Uke's* face (photo #2). Cutting downward on inside of *Uke's* arm while engaging hips to rear, *Nage* breaks *Uke's* balance (photo #3). Taking control of *Uke's* wrist, *Nage* solidly rotates hips toward *Uke* while securing grip on elbow with right hand (photo #4).

2

3

4

5

6

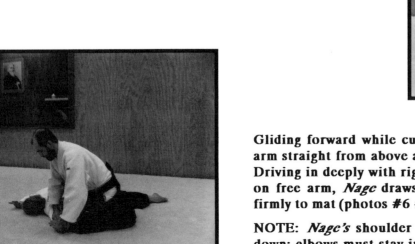

7

Gliding forward while cutting fully, *Nage* holds *Uke's* arm straight from above and behind elbow (photo #5). Driving in deeply with right foot, placing *Uke's* weight on free arm, *Nage* draws up back foot and pins *Uke* firmly to mat (photos #6 #7), see *Katame Waza* section.

NOTE: *Nage's* shoulder and hip power must remain down; elbows must stay in alignment with hips and not be allowed to turn outward.

KATATETORI IKKYO *TENKAN/URA*

Uke utilizes straight hand grab from *Gyaku-Hanmi* (photo #1).

APPLIED PRINCIPLES: Moving sharply 90 degrees to left, *Nage* directs *Atemi* to *Uke's* face with right hand, making sure to keep left hand (held hand) centered with hips (photo #2). Bringing right forearm heavily down *Uke's* arm to elbow while gliding back engaging hips, *Nage* breaks *Uke's* balance (photos #3 #4).

1

2

3

4

5

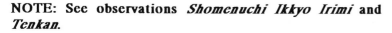

6

Taking firm hold of *Uke's* wrist, *Nage* rotates left hip inward while stepping forward to align left foot with *Uke* (photo #5). Throwing right foot back 90 degrees while rotating hips powerfully clockwise, *Nage* lowers hips to firmly pin *Uke* (photos #6 #7).

NOTE: See observations *Shomenuchi Ikkyo Irimi* and *Tenkan.*

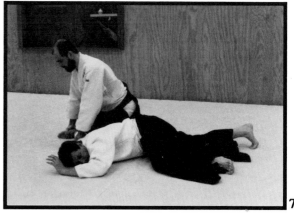

7

YOKOMENUCHI IKKYO *TENKAN/URA*

1

Uke utilizes strike to side of head from *Ai-Hanmi* (photo #1).

APPLIED PRINCIPLES: Gliding powerfully forward, *Nage* stops *Uke's* arm before it passes mid point of swing, simultaneously driving *Atemi* to face with right hand (photo #2). Cutting *Uke's* arm toward center with right hand, *Nage* aligns posture (photo #3).

2

3

4

5

6

Throwing right leg back, *Nage* rotates hips drawing *Uke* sharply around (photos #4 #5). Lowering hips firmly, *Nage* pins *Uke* to mat (photo #6).

NOTE: This *Waza* demonstrates a varied takedown which may be utilized with assorted *Ikkyo Tenkan*. To apply variation, *Uke's* wrist is pinned at *Nage's* hip during rotation (photo #5) while driving *Uke* to mat with pressure administered directly downward through arm to shoulder for pin.

RYOTEMOCHI IKKYO *IRIMI / OMOTE*

Uke utilizes a two hands on one wrist hold from *Gyaku-Hanmi* (photo #1).

APPLIED PRINCIPLES: Gliding forward and to the outside while pivoting powerfully and lowering hips, *Nage* aligns with initial direction (photo #2).

Throwing right foot back 180 degrees, *Nage* draws *Uke's* balance forward and around (photo #3). Gliding forward with left foot, *Nage* cuts left hand over *Uke's* left wrist while taking elbow with right hand and rotates hips fully, cutting downward (photos #4 #5). Stepping deeply forward with right foot, *Nage* then draws in left foot and pins *Uke* to mat (photos #6 #7).

USHIRO RYOKATATORI IKKYO *IRIMI/OMOTE*

1

Uke utilizes two rear shoulder grab (photo #1).

APPLIED PRINCIPLES: Lowering hips while gliding back and under *Uke's* left arm, *Nage* breaks the plane of *Uke's* posture (photo #2). Positioning right hand just above elbow, *Nage* rotates hips powerfully toward *Uke*, causing *Uke's* weight to shift to his outer foot (close-up photo). Reaching up to take *Uke's* wrist with left hand (palm upward with thumb facing away from *Uke*), *Nage* simultaneously cuts sharply downward during completion of hip rotation (photos #3 #4). Driving right hip and foot forward into *Uke's* center, *Nage* draws left foot in and pins *Uke* firmly to mat (photos #5 #6).

2

3

6

4

5

NOTE: *Nage's* back must remain straight during *Waza*. *Atemi* may be employed to face and groin simultaneously (photo #2).

OBSERVATION: *Nage* should have the feeling of a powerful wave breaking first under then over the hapless *Uke*.

TSUKI IKKYO _TENKAN/URA_

1

Uke utilizes thrusting attack from _Ai-Hanmi_ (photo #1).

APPLIED PRINCIPLES: Stepping forward and to the inside of _Uke's_ thrust, _Nage_ takes _Uke's_ wrist with right hand (photo #2).

2

3

4

5

Raising _Uke's_ arm, _Nage_ controls elbow from below while stepping forward aligning left foot with _Uke's_ right foot (photo #3). Throwing right foot back, _Nage_ rotates hips drawing _Uke_ sharply around (photos #4 #5). Lowering hips firmly, _Nage_ pins _Uke_ to mat (photo #6).

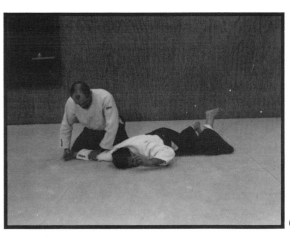

6

NIKYO

(SECOND TEACHING)

Literally translated as "second teaching," *Nikyo* refers to the second control technique taught in the sequence of *Ikkyo* through *Gokyo*. Though capable of generating immense pain, the essence of *Nikyo* lies in *Nage's* ability to restrain the muscular, skeletal, and spiritual movement of *Uke* while utilizing *Uke's* own *Tegatana* (handblade/sword) to figuratively sever *Uke* in two. *Nikyo* deserves and demands close and diligent study.

KATATETORI NIKYO *IRIMI / OMOTE*

Uke utilizes straight hand grab from *Gyaku-Hanmi* (photo #1).

NOTE: *Uke* should not stand square to *Nage*, nor vice-versa. To do so is to allow a *Suki* (opening). This principle is integral to all *Waza*.

APPLIED PRINCIPLES: Moving sharply 90 degrees to the left, *Nage* directs *Atemi* toward *Uke's* face while making sure to keep left hand centered with hips (photo #2).

NOTE: During *Hanmi* change and realignment of forward foot, *Nage* must move *Uke's* arm in a smooth arc, generating power through the function of integrated body movement emanating from hips.

Taking control of *Uke's* wrist with right hand while rotating hips powerfully toward *Uke*, *Nage* glides forward raising arm, then cutting fully downward, locking arm firmly in place with left hand at elbow (photo #3).

NOTE: At this point pressure may be applied to the base of *Uke's* index and middle knuckles on back of hand using *Yonkyo* applied *Ken* grip (see *Yonkyo* section).

Stepping forward with left foot, *Nage* thrusts hip deeply into *Uke's* center, causing *Uke* to lose balance and use free arm for support (photo # 4).

NOTE: At this point, *Uke* may also be pinned with *Ikkyo Irimi*.

Releasing *Uke's* elbow, *Nage* brings wrist quickly to left shoulder, pinning the circle of *Uke's* thumb and forefinger to a point just below collarbone (photo #5).

NOTE: See close-up *Ryokatatori Nikyo*. *Nage's* left elbow controls *Uke's* elbow bend. *Nage's* left hand encircles *Uke's* right wrist.

Drawing in elbow, *Nage* bows forward, directing *Uke's* fingers toward his face while simultaneously stepping slightly back and engaging hips fully into movement (photo #6).

OBSERVATION: *Nikyo* teaches us about human frailties. *Nikyo* should not be performed with a malicious heart.

Releasing left wrist hold, *Nage* controls *Uke's* elbow from behind while stepping forward with right foot to pin *Uke* to mat. Pivoting right knee to mat, *Nage* straddles *Uke's* shoulder and applies ending (photos #7 #8). See section on *Katame Waza* (formal endings).

SHOMENUCHI NIKYO *TENKAN/URA*

1

Uke utilizes overhead strike from *Gyaku-Hanmi* (photo #1).

APPLIED PRINCIPLES: Stepping forward and to the outside, *Nage* aligns left foot with *Uke's* right foot simultaneously meeting *Uke's* attacking arm with right *Tegatana* (handblade) and taking control of wrist with left hand (photos #2 #3).

2

NOTE: Above photo shows close-up of control movements in photos #2 #3.

3

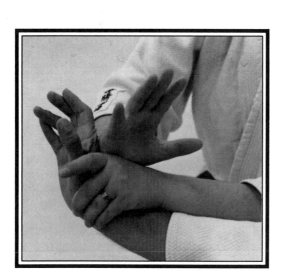

4

Throwing right foot back 90 degrees, *Nage* cuts *Uke's* arm into center. Rotating *Uke's* hand so that thumb is pointing downward, *Nage* inserts right thumb between thumb and index finger of *Uke's* hand to take *Ken* grip (photo #4).

5

Keeping weight forward, *Nage* powerfully draws *Uke's* wrist up to collarbone area (see close-up *Ryokatatori Nikyo*). Controlling elbow, *Nage* rotates hips so that wrist points toward *Uke's* center (photo #5).

Drawing elbow in and bowing forward, *Nage* points *Uke's* fingers toward *Uke* while stepping slightly back and engaging hips fully into movement (photo #6).

6

Releasing left wrist hold, *Nage* takes control of elbow from behind while pivoting 180 degrees to firmly pin *Uke* to mat (photo #7).

NOTE: In performing *Tenkan Waza*, *Nage* may pin to the rear in various degrees; 45, 180, 270, etc. as needed.

7

Keeping elbow bent, *Nage* pivots right knee to mat straddling *Uke's* shoulder and applies ending (photo #8). See section on *Katame Waza* (formal endings).

OBSERVATION: Although *Nikyo* should be applied with overwhelming authority, as that of a falcon clutching prey within its talons, it is usually *Uke's* continued resistance to blame for injuries suffered during training.

8

YOKOMENUCHI NIKYO *IRIMI/OMOTE*

Uke utilizes strike to side of head from *Ai-Hanmi* (photo #1).

APPLIED PRINCIPLES: Gliding powerfully forward, *Nage* stops attack before it reaches midpoint while driving *Atemi* to *Uke's* face (photo #2). See *Yokomenuchi Sankyo* final note.

Cutting *Uke's* arm toward center with left arm, *Nage* takes control of elbow while breaking *Uke's* balance forward (photo #3). Rotating left thumb across back of *Uke's* hand, *Nage* drives right foot toward *Uke* while taking *Nikyo* grip (photos #4 #5). Drawing *Uke's* wrist to right shoulder, *Nage* applies *Nikyo* (photos #6 #7).

RYOKATATORI NIKYO

Uke utilizes a two lapel grab from *Ai-Hanmi* (photo #1).

APPLIED PRINCIPLES: Stepping deeply to left side, *Nage* brings right arm over *Uke's* grab while cutting downward and drawing hips sharply to rear, breaking *Uke's* balance (photo #2).

Locking *Uke's* right hand to shoulder with *Nikyo* (see close-up photo below) while trapping left hand beneath elbow, *Nage* steps forward and aligns left foot with *Uke's* center (photo #3).

Locking *Uke's* right elbow to ribcage, *Nage* simultaneously steps slightly back with right foot and engages both hips, applying *Nikyo* control (photo #4). *Nage* may then choose to pin with *Irimi* or *Tenkan Katame Waza*.

NOTE: *Uke's* arm is locked from inner knuckle of index finger and thumb, downward through wrist and forearm to elbow, secured firmly against *Nage's* upper torso.

TSUKI NIKYO

1

Uke utilizes a thrusting attack from *Ai-Hanmi* (photo #1).

APPLIED PRINCIPLES: Stepping forward and to the inside of *Uke*, *Nage* strikes attacking wrist (photo #2).

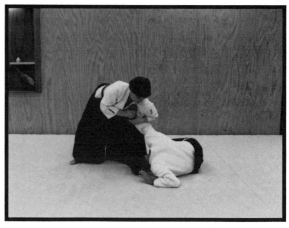

2

3

4

Taking *Nikyo* grip with right hand, *Nage* steps forward rotating *Uke's* little finger toward his face and aligns left foot with *Uke's* right foot (photo #3). Sliding right foot back slightly, *Nage* engages hips and applies *Nikyo* (photos #4 #5). *Nage* may then choose to pin with *Irimi* or *Tenkan Katame Waza*.

5

HANTAI NIKYO

1

Uke utilizes a cross hand grab from *Ai-Hanmi* (photo #1).

APPLIED PRINCIPLES: Raising both arms with strong *Kokyu* power, *Nage* glides forward and to the outside while trapping *Uke's* fingers to right forearm with left palm (photo #2).

2

3

4

Cutting right hand above *Uke's* wrist, *Nage* moves left leg into newly created center line at a 45 degree angle to *Uke's* right side (photo #3). Continuing circular cut back and into *Uke's* center, *Nage* folds right wrist sharply over *Uke's* forearm, driving *Uke* to mat (photo #4). See close-up sequence on next page.

NOTE: It is important that the angle of initial movement (photo #2) does not expose *Nage's* back to *Uke*. *Nage's* hands and *Uke's* grab should remain clearly between partners throughout execution of *Waza*.

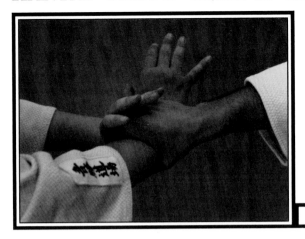

Nage must firmly secure bottom two thirds of *Uke's* fingers with heel portion of palm so that *Uke* will not be able to loosen grip (photo #1, top of page). If focus of hold is to the back of *Uke's* hand, *Uke* will be able to straighten fingers and jerk hand free of grip.

Continuing circle up from point of origin, *Nage* cuts sharply across *Uke's* wrist at point of bend, moving *Tegatana* (handblade, small finger side of hand from tip to elbow) as though cutting hand free from wrist at joint (photo #2, center of page).

Folding sharply over wrist (full hand including thumb), *Nage* applies flow of energy downward completing full circle of hand movement. Care should be taken to create a bend in, and fully control *Uke's* elbow. Placing *Uke's* arm in this configuration allows *Nage* to control *Uke's* movement to front and rear (photo #3, bottom of page).

1

2

3

Uke utilizes two rear elbow grab (photo #1).

APPLIED PRINCIPLES: Raising both arms while rolling forearms forward, causing *Uke's* elbows to open outward, *Nage* lowers hips and glides back and under *Uke's* left arm (photo #2). Trapping the fingers of *Uke's* right hand to elbow with heel of left palm (see close-up sequence *Hantai Nikyo*), *Nage* steps back with right foot and drives right forearm over *Uke's* right arm (photo #3). Focusing energy downward, *Nage* takes *Uke* to mat (photo #4). Releasing fingers with left hand, *Nage* takes control of underside of *Uke's* elbow while moving right hand to grip *Uke's* wrist. Stepping forward with right foot, *Nage* prepares to move *Uke* into a prone position for ending (photo #5). See *Katatetori Nikyo* for ending sequence.

4

NOTE: *Nage* should not attempt to force *Uke's* elbow down with right hand when applying *Nikyo* (photo #4). Application of smooth semi-circular pressure downward at point on forearm just above wrist will cause painful musculo-skeletal compliance with very little effort on *Nage's* part.

5

SANKYO

(THIRD TEACHING)

Literally translated as "third teaching," *Sankyo* refers to the third control technique taught in the sequence of *Ikkyo* through *Gokyo*. As with all controlling technique within the body of *Aikido*, *Sankyo* teaches us to take control of *Uke's* entire body. When applying *Sankyo* to the left wrist, we must seek to control *Uke's* right toes while at the same time taking a firm grasp of *Uke's* aggressive spirit. The spherical and spiral motion of *Sankyo* allows us to cut around *Uke's* strong points and slip powerfully into his/her center. Once a good deal of familiarity of its *Kihon* (basic) form has been acquired, *Sankyo* provides an opportunity for free and rapid movement into techniques including *Kokyu-Nage*, *Irimi-Nage*, and *Shiho-Nage*.

SHOMENUCHI SANKYO *IRIMI / OMOTE*

1

Uke utilizes overhead strike, stepping forward from *Gyaku-Hanmi* (photo #1).

APPLIED PRINCIPLES: *Nage* glides powerfully forward, utilizing *Ikkyo Waza* for initial control (photos #2 #3 #4). See *Shomenuchi Ikkyo Irimi.*

2

3

4

Aligning hips at *Uke's* side, *Nage* releases elbow hold and bows shoulder forward to prevent *Uke* from regaining balance while moving right hand to control with *Sankyo* (photos #5 & close-up below).

5

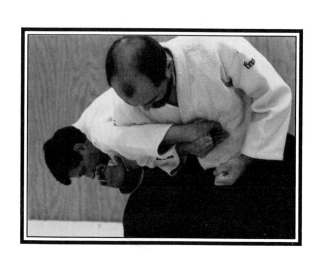

6

Keeping *Sankyo* locked at solar plexis, *Nage* steps forward with left foot applying *Atemi* with left hand to *Uke's* face (photo #6). *Nage* rotates hips and throws right leg back clockwise away from *Uke*, while cutting strongly to center and controlling elbow with left hand (photo #7).

7

8

Stepping back and kneeling with left leg *Nage* pins *Uke* to mat (photo #8). Changing hands but not losing *Sankyo* hold, *Nage* moves into *Seiza* while locking *Uke's* arm to chest. Applying rotation toward *Uke's* head, *Nage* concentrates on pinning the triangular area of *Uke's* breastbone just below the throat firmly to the mat (photo #9). See *Katame Waza* section.

9

YOKOMENUCHI SANKYO *TENKAN / URA*

Uke utilizes strike to side of head from *Ai-Hanmi* (photo #1).

APPLIED PRINCIPLES: As *Uke* steps forward with attack, *Nage* glides forcefully to the outside, stopping *Uke's* arm before it gains full momentum (photo #2).

NOTE: *Nage's* position should allow *Atemi* to be applied to *Uke's* face, making it necessary for *Uke* to step forward with left foot in order to strike *Nage*.

Bringing right hand over left forearm (see footnote on next page), *Nage* cuts arm toward *Uke*, placing elbow on original line of *Uke's* spine. Controlling with *Ikkyo*, *Nage* throws right foot back 180 degrees (photos #3 #4).

NOTE: At this point *Nage* may choose to step forward with right leg and apply *Irimi Waza* (photo #3 #4). See *Shomenuchi Sankyo Irimi.*

Taking *Sankyo*, *Nage* rotates wrist counterclockwise toward *Uke* while driving elbow upward (photo #5). Simultaneously stepping behind *Uke* with left foot and cutting downward, *Nage* takes control of *Uke's* elbow (photo #6).

7

Stepping back with right foot, *Nage* pins *Uke* and performs seated *Katame Waza* (photos #7 #8). See *Ushiro Kubishime Sankyo* for sequence.

8

INCORRECT   **COUNTER**   **CORRECT**

NOTE: It is of utmost importance that *Nage* does not lift elbow when bringing hand across forearm (left photo, incorrect). If this is done, it will allow an opening for *Uke* to counter the *Waza* with *Ikkyo* etc. or strike to *Nage's* ribcage (center photo, counter). When done correctly, *Nage* keeps elbows down (below shoulders) and commands *Uke's* center (right photo, correct), keeping *Uke* off balance.

POSTNOTE: DO NOT bring free arm under blocking arm. This traps blocking arm and removes focus from *Uke*. When correctly brought over forearm, it will allow *Nage* to keep *Uke's* balance under control and counter any movements with either *Atemi* or by driving elbow upward to break *Uke's* arm.

Uke utilizes a two rear wrist hold (photo #1).

APPLIED PRINCIPLES: Raising both arms with strong *Kokyu* power while keeping elbows close to body (causing *Uke's* elbows to remain outside), *Nage* glides back and under *Uke's* right arm, lowering body with knees, not by bending forward (photo #2). *Nage* then takes a step back with left foot and controls with *Ikkyo* (photo #3).

Stepping in with left foot, *Nage* drives *Uke* further off balance (photo #4). Releasing elbow and taking *Sankyo* hold, *Nage* rotates wrist upward in a counterclockwise spiral directly over forward foot, as if raising *Ken* (photo # 5).

Taking a half step behind *Uke* with left foot and throwing right foot back 45 degrees, *Nage* pins *Uke* and applies seated ending (photos #6 #7). See *Oyo Waza* on next page (photos #6 #7 #8) for *Katame Waza* (formal ending) sequence.

OYO WAZA

1

2

One of many variations of *Ushiro Tori Sankyo*, this *Oyo Waza* is applied by *Nage* maintaining a left *Hanmi* (photos #1 #2 #3), immediately taking *Sankyo* grip, and combining step back with pinning action (photos #4 #5 #6 #7 #8).

3

4

5

6

7

8

NOTE: Photos #6 #7 #8 show sequential application of *Sankyo Katame Waza* as applied in either *Tenkan* or *Irimi*.

USHIRO KUBISHIME SANKYO *TENKAN / URA*

1

Uke utilizes a wrist and one arm strangle hold from rear.

APPLIED PRINCIPLES: As *Uke's* arm encircles neck, *Nage* must lock into a strong posture: chin down and center thrust back against *Uke* to unstable his attack (photo #1).

2

3

4

Reaching up with right hand to lock arm to chest, *Nage* turns head toward bend at *Uke's* elbow while stepping out 45 degrees with left foot (photos #2 #3). Releasing elbow and taking *Uke's* left hand, *Nage* applies *Sankyo* to free left wrist (photo #4), and takes *Uke's* fingers in *Ken* grip (close-up photo).

NOTE: *Uke's* grabbing arm is locked above *Nage's* by upward pressure to back of elbow (close-up photo). If *Uke* releases grip, *Nage* cuts instantly and pins with *Tenkan Waza*. If *Uke* holds, *Nage* cuts rigorously downward while turning 180 degrees clockwise toward *Uke* and pins with *Irimi Waza*. This rotation causes *Uke's* left shoulder to cut his arm from *Nage's* lapel.

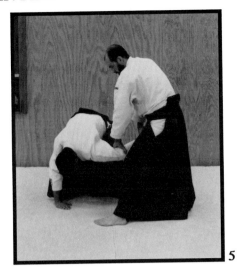

5

Taking a half step behind *Uke* with right foot, *Nage* then controls elbow with left hand (photo #5). Stepping back with left foot, *Nage* sinks knee, hip, and held elbow combination firmly to mat, pinning *Uke's* shoulder and collar bone region (photo #6).

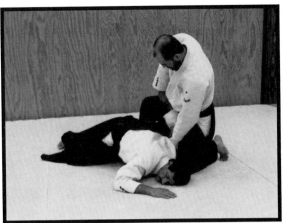

6

OBSERVATION: As with a table having four legs, once one is removed it is not wise to place your dinner at that location since you will most definitely disrupt the integrity of the table, not to mention your meal. Within *Ikkyo* through *Gokyo Waza* it is necessary for *Nage* to be sure that *Uke's* table is cluttered so he must rely on this weak corner.

7

Exchanging hands but retaining *Sankyo* grip, *Nage* brings right knee down to straddle *Uke's* shoulder (photos #7 #8). *Nage* rotates posture toward and over *Uke's* head, concentrating on pinning the triangular area of *Uke's* breastbone just below the throat securely to the mat.

NOTE: See *Katame Waza* section for possible *Oyo-Katame* (varied ending) applications.

8

YONKYO

(FOURTH TEACHING)

Literally translated as "fourth teaching," *Yonkyo* refers to the fourth control technique taught in the sequence of *Ikkyo* through *Gokyo*. Most commonly referring to the pressure applied against general nerves running along the radius bone of the forearm, *Yonkyo* may also be applied to various other parts of the body such as the ankle, shin, and neck. The basis for a compelling *Yonkyo* comes from the development of a concentrated *Ken* grip. It has been said that *O'Sensei's* grip was such that it would leave hand-shaped bruises on the wrists of his partners. Daily practice of *Tanren-Uchi* (see *Ken* section) can prove to be an invaluable factor in the development of a strong *Ken* grip, the importance of which will become unmistakably evident during the practice of *Yonkyo*.

SHOMENUCHI YONKYO *IRIMI/OMOTE*

Uke utilizes overhead strike from *Gyaku-Hanmi* (photo #1).

APPLIED PRINCIPLES: *Nage* glides powerfully forward and applies *Ikkyo Irimi* (photos #2 #3 #4), see *Shomenuchi Ikkyo Irimi*. Bending *Uke's* elbow and sliding right hand to inside of forearm, *Nage* secures firm *Yonkyo* grip (see close-up, *Hantai Yonkyo Irimi*) and drives *Uke* into the mat for *Irimi* pin (photos #5 #6).

Continuing nerve pressure, *Nage* places knee into *Uke's* armpit while driving elbow toward heel of forward foot (photo #7).

SHOMENUCHI YONKYO *TENKAN/URA*

1

Uke utilizes overhead strike from *Gyaku-Hanmi* (photo #1).

APPLIED PRINCIPLES: Driving in and to the outside, *Nage* aligns with *Uke's* forward foot while taking control of elbow. Then directing wrist, *Nage* applies basic *Ikkyo Tenkan* (photos #2 #3 #4), see *Shomenuchi Ikkyo Tenkan*.

2

Bending *Uke's* arm and driving him to the mat, *Nage* slips left hand inside of arm to apply nerve hold to wrist (photo #5). Using momentum caused by nerve pressure, *Nage* pivots hips while pointing *Uke's* elbow to mat for *Tenkan* pin. Placing left knee in armpit, *Nage* applies ending by continuing nerve pressure while driving elbow toward heel of forward foot (photo #6).

NOTE: *Yonkyo* is applied by using *Ken* grip with inside of index finger's base knuckle pressed against the inside of *Uke's* radius bone just above the wrist.

3

4

5

6

HANTAI YONKYO *IRIMI/OMOTE*

Uke utilizes a cross hand grab from *Ai-Hanmi* (photo #1).

APPLIED PRINCIPLES: Driving left *Tegatana* up and over the outside of *Uke's* left wrist, *Nage* takes control of elbow from below and applies *Ikkyo Irimi* (photos #2 #3).

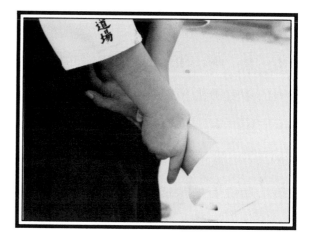

Bending *Uke's* arm at elbow, *Nage* applies *Yonkyo* grip (photo #4). Performing *Irimi Waza*, *Nage* drives *Uke* to the mat, advances left foot and pins (photo #5).

NOTE: In *Ken* gripping application of *Yonkyo*, inside hand (closest to *Uke*) is always high with outside hand lower (close-up photo).

USHIRO TORI YONKYO *TENKAN / URA*

1

Uke attempts the utilization of a full nelson attack (photo #1).

APPLIED PRINCIPLES: Dropping center with elbows and shoulders locked down, *Nage* reaches up and takes *Uke's* little fingers. Turning hands out and down, *Nage* releases right hand and pivots sharply back on *Uke* (photos #2 #3 #4 #5).

2

3

4

5

6

Applying *Ikkyo Tenkan* then *Yonkyo*, *Nage* pins *Uke* securely to mat (photos #6 #7 #8).

7

8

RYOTEMOCHI YONKYO *TENKAN/URA*

1

Uke utilizes a two hands on one wrist hold from *Gyaku-Hanmi* (photo #1).

APPLIED PRINCIPLES: Gliding forward and to the outside, *Nage* powerfully rotates and lowers hips while aligning with *Uke's* direction (photo #2). Throwing right foot back 180 degrees, *Nage* draws *Uke's* balance forward and around (photo #3).

2

3

4

5

Stepping back with left foot, *Nage* applies *Atemi* to face with right hand (photo #4). Using right hand, *Nage* peels *Uke's* right hand free while stepping forward to control elbow and align left foot (photo #5). Throwing right foot back, *Nage* cuts *Uke* down and onto free arm (photo #6).

6

7

8

9

10

Taking *Yonkyo* grip with left hand, *Nage* drives *Uke* to mat (photo #7). Placing left knee deeply into *Uke's* armpit while placing right foot forward and to the outside of *Uke's* shoulder, *Nage* drives hips forward directing *Uke's* elbow toward heel of raised foot to implement basic pin (photo #8). See note below.

NOTE: The final three photos demonstrate three *Oyo-* (varied) *Katame Waza*: elbow lock with heel assistance (photo #9), free heel lock (photo #10), and heel lock with opposite arm entrapment (photo #11).

11

GOKYO

(FIFTH TEACHING)

Literally translated as "fifth teaching," *Gokyo* refers to the fifth control technique taught in the sequence of *Ikkyo* through *Gokyo*. Utilized primarily to control *Uke's* knife or sword-wielding arm (see *Tanto Tori* for additional *Gokyo* applications), the practice of *Gokyo* as an unarmed discipline should by no means be overlooked. Though at first glance *Gokyo* may appear to be identical to *Ikkyo* (physically differentiated only by the reversed gripping position of the outer hand), this is definitely not the case. The controlling factors of *Gokyo* allow for both forward and lateral pressure during application. It should also be noted that even when applying *Gokyo* in its *Irimi* form, *Nage's* initial entry is to the outside of *Uke's* posture. The sizable challenge presented by the study of *Gokyo* can only be met through frequent and exacting effort.

OBSERVATION: Lately, a disturbing trend has surfaced in which a number of *Aikido* instructors have chosen to eliminate *Gokyo* from their criteria, shockingly even in the application of *Tanto Tori* (knife taking). The obvious error behind this exclusion should serve to drive those of us practicing *Aikido* in its traditional state even deeper into our personal study of the scope of *Gokyo*.

SHOMENUCHI GOKYO *IRIMI / OMOTE*

Uke utilizes overhead strike from *Gyaku-Hanmi* (photo #1).

APPLIED PRINCIPLES: Stepping forward and to the outside, *Nage* aligns left foot with *Uke's* right foot while simultaneously taking control of attacking arm at point just below elbow (photo #2).

Delivering *Atemi* to ribs with right hand, *Nage* drives *Uke's* elbow onto line of spine, breaking *Uke's* balance (photo #3). Reaching up to take firm grasp of *Uke's* wrist with right hand, *Nage* drives in and across *Uke's* front with right foot (photo #4).

NOTE: *Atemi* is applied with middle knuckle protruding fist (photo #3). Hand which applies *Atemi* then moves to grasp wrist, keeping palm upward with thumb closest to *Nage* (photo #4).

CONTINUED ☞

Rotating hips powerfully clockwise, *Nage* cuts *Uke's* balance sharply forward (photo #5). Stepping in deeply with left foot, *Nage* drives *Uke* onto left elbow (photo #6). Drawing right leg forward, *Nage* firmly lowers hips, pinning *Uke* to mat (photo #7).

NOTE: To apply *Gokyo* correctly, *Nage* must be sure to keep outer wrist (hand at *Uke's* wrist) in a straight and locked position while keeping the palm in full and secure contact with *Uke's* wrist (photos #4 #5 #6 #7).

Applying *Yonkyo* pressure (see *Yonkyo* section) to point at separation of wrist and forearm, *Nage* draws *Uke's* wrist in and underneath elbow. Pressing squarely on back of elbow, *Nage* concentrates energy downward toward inner knuckles of open palm (photo #8).

SHOMENUCHI GOKYO *TENKAN / URA*

Uke utilizes overhead strike from *Gyaku-Hanmi* (photo #1).

APPLIED PRINCIPLES: Stepping forward and to the outside aligning right foot with *Uke's* left foot, *Nage* applies *Atemi* to ribs with left fist while taking control of *Uke's* attacking arm at point just below elbow, breaking *Uke's* balance (photo #2).

Reaching up with left hand, *Nage* takes control of *Uke's* wrist by gripping with palm upward and thumb toward *Nage* (photo #3). Throwing left foot back, *Nage* rotates hips sharply counterclockwise, cutting *Uke* in a circle downward (photo #4). Lowering hips powerfully, *Nage* pins *Uke* to mat (photo #5). Driving wrist up and underneath elbow, *Nage* applies *Gokyo* ending (photo #6). See *Gokyo Irimi* for ending sequence.

SHIHO-NAGE
(FOUR DIRECTION THROW)

Literally translated as "four direction throw," *Shiho-Nage* allows for the projection of *Uke* into essentially any point of the spectrum, i.e. if you have four directions, you have the possibility of eight, sixteen etc., etc. As with virtually all *Waza* (technique) within the body of *Aikido*, *Shiho-Nage* can be traced to methods developed by the *Bushi* (warrior caste) for utilization against sword or spear-wielding opponents. Having been stated on a number of occasions that *O'Sensei* would frequently scold his *Uchi-Deshi* (inside students) for not having practiced *Shiho-Nage* daily, we should remain ever mindful of the importance placed on *Shiho-Nage* by *O'Sensei* and pursue a constant endeavor to bring about a greater understanding of this significant *Waza*.

KATATETORI SHIHO-NAGE *IRIMI/OMOTE*

Uke utilizes straight hand grab from *Gyaku-Hanmi* (photo #1).

APPLIED PRINCIPLES: Offsetting right foot directly to side while placing left foot under grabbed hand, *Nage* reaches over *Uke's* wrist and takes *Ken* grip (photo #2). Stepping forward with right foot, *Nage* frees grabbed hand and pivots immediately back to *Uke's* shoulder (photo #3).

Cutting down fully with both hands to *Uke's* left rear corner with slight hip rotation, *Nage* executes throw as though cutting deeply with *Ken* to point just inside of forward foot (photos #4 #5).

KATATETORI SHIHO-NAGE *TENKAN / URA*

Uke utilizes straight hand grab from *Gyaku-Hanmi* (photo #1).

APPLIED PRINCIPLES: Gliding forward, placing left foot at *Uke's* right, *Nage* aligns shoulder while taking *Ken* grip on *Uke's* right hand (photo #2 & close-up).

Throwing right foot back, *Nage* drives wrist to *Uke's* shoulder and cuts fully for throw (photos #3 #4 #5). *Nage* moves left foot back to *Uke's* side and applies standing *Katame Waza* by continuing *Shiho* rotation while pressing forearm to *Uke's* tricep area, pinning head and opposite shoulder to mat (photo #6).

YOKOMENUCHI SHIHO-NAGE *IRIMI | OMOTE*

Uke utilizes a side strike to the head from *Ai-Hanmi* (photo #1).

APPLIED PRINCIPLES: Stepping forward and to the inside of *Uke*, *Nage* deflects strike out and down with right forearm, while applying *Atemi* with left hand (photo #2).

OBSERVATION: *Uke's* attacking hand is only the effect, whereas his *Chushin* (centerline) is the cause. You will not be able to handle *Uke* until you have broken his *Kime* (focus) and have full control of his balance, just as you cannot stop missiles from being fired at you until you effectively disrupt their base of operations.

Taking attacking hand from beneath with left hand, *Nage* steps back with right foot and completes *Hanmi* change (photo #3).

NOTE: At this point *Nage* may decide to apply *Tenkan Waza* by stepping to *Uke's* left side with right foot (see *Katatetori Shiho-Nage Tenkan*), or *Irimi Waza* as described below.

First taking a glide step forward with left foot, then a deep step forward with right, *Nage* begins to pivot hips (photo #4).

NOTE: *Nage* keeps buttocks toward *Uke* with knees bent and back rounded. *Uke's* hand should be held solidly to the front of *Nage's* head at all times and not be permitted to go behind head during pivot.

5

Completing sharp pivot and driving *Uke's* wrist in and below his shoulder, while maintaining full control of *Uke's* balance, *Nage* cuts fully to point just inside of forward foot (photos #5 #6 #7). See *Ken Suburi* section (cutting with sword).

6

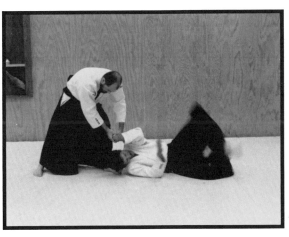

7

Placing weight forward on *Uke*, *Nage* continues to curl wrist to shoulder while throwing right foot back to align with *Uke's* left side. Driving left forearm into *Uke's* tricep area, *Nage* pins head and opposite shoulder to mat (photo #8). See *Katame Waza* section for *Oyo-Katame* (varied pins).

8

SHOMENUCHI SHIHO-NAGE *IRIMI/OMOTE*

1

APPLIED PRINCIPLES: Taking the initiative, *Nage* drives left *Tegatana* (handblade) toward *Uke's* face, causing *Uke* to reflect (*Suigetsu*-moon on water) the motion (photos #1 #2). Shifting right foot to a 90 degree angle, *Nage* takes *Uke's* balance by cutting right forearm over left, taking *Uke's* left wrist (photos #3 #4).

2

3

4

5

6

7

Nage then performs *Shiho-Nage Irimi* (shown, photos #5 #6 #7) or *Tenkan*, see *Katatetori Shiho-Nage Irimi* and *Tenkan*.

USHIRO RYOTETORI SHIHO-NAGE IRIMI/OMOTE

1

Uke utilizes a two rear wrist hold (photo #1).

APPLIED PRINCIPLES: Using strong *Kokyu* power, *Nage* raises both arms while stepping back and under *Uke's* left arm (photo #2).

Turning right palm up, *Nage* draws *Uke's* right wrist across chest while taking firm *Ken* grip (photo #3).

2

3

4

5

6

Stepping forward with left foot, *Nage* pivots sharply back to shoulder and cuts fully (photos #4 #5 #6 #7 #8). See *Katatetori Shiho-Nage Irimi.*

7

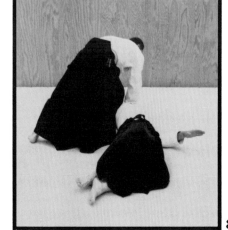

8

NOTE: *Nage* may step with left foot to right side and perform *Tenkan Waza* (photo #3). See *Katatetori Shiho-Nage Tenkan.*

135

RYOTEMOCHI SHIHO-NAGE *IRIMI/OMOTE*

Uke utilizes a two hands on one wrist hold from *Gyaku-Hanmi* (photo #1).

APPLIED PRINCIPLES: Gliding forward and to the outside, *Nage* rotates and lowers hips to align with *Uke's* initial direction (photo #2). Throwing left foot back 180 degrees, *Nage* draws *Uke* around while cutting right arm into center (photo #3).

Bringing left hand to *Uke's* elbow, *Nage* places inside knuckle of index finger (thumb pointing upward) against outside of elbow and rotates hips powerfully clockwise, driving *Uke's* right arm beneath his left while taking *Shiho-Nage* grip with right hand (photo #4). Stepping forward with left foot, *Nage* pivots sharply back to *Uke's* shoulder (photo #5). Cutting downward to point just inside of forward foot, *Nage* executes throw (photo #6).

136

KATATORI SHOMENUCHI SHIHO-NAGE *IRIMI / OMOTE*

Uke utilizes one lapel/shoulder grab from *Gyaku-Hanmi* (photo #1).

APPLIED PRINCIPLES: Gliding straight in, *Nage* strikes with *Tegatana Atemi* causing *Uke* to block with right hand (photo #2). At point of contact, *Nage* suddenly throws left foot back while cutting downward, drawing *Uke* forward (photo #3).

Stepping back with right foot while drawing *Uke's* right arm through, *Nage* takes *Shiho-Nage* grip with both hands. Rotating hips powerfully clockwise, *Nage* directs head beneath *Uke's* left arm (photo #4). Stepping forward with left foot, *Nage* pivots sharply back to *Uke's* shoulder, executing throw by cutting fully to point just inside of forward foot (photos #5 #6).

KATATORI SHIHO-NAGE *IRIMI/OMOTE*

1

Uke utilizes one lapel/shoulder grab from *Gyaku-Hanmi* (photo #1).

2

3

4

APPLIED PRINCIPLES: Moving sharply 90 degrees to the outside, simultaneously changing to a left *Hanmi* and lowering hips, *Nage* drives *Atemi* toward *Uke's* face (photo #2). Taking *Shiho-Nage* grip with both hands, *Nage* holds *Uke's* wrist firmly at lapel. Rotating hips slightly clockwise while dropping head and right shoulder over wrist to the outside, *Nage* then rotates hips powerfully counterclockwise toward *Uke* while driving shoulder upward causing *Uke* to raise onto toes (photo #3). Stepping forward with right foot, *Nage* pivots sharply back to *Uke's* shoulder while placing right knee on mat (photo #4). Driving forward onto left knee, *Nage* cuts powerfully to point just inside of knee while drawing right foot and knee forward, executing throw (photo #5).

NOTE: Demonstrated here as a *Tachi Waza* to *Hanmi-Handachi Waza* (standing moving to half standing - half seated) application, this *Shiho-Nage*, as well as many other *Waza*, may also be performed as *Suwari Waza* to *Tachi Waza* (seated moving to a standing position).

5

SHIHO-NAGE *RIAI - INTERRELATIONSHIP*

On this and the next two pages are examples of the physical interrelationship of *Ken* and *Jo* to *Taijutsu* (empty-handed body arts) as manifested within the *Riai* of *Aikido*. It is said that virtually all *Taijutsu*, on a physical level, may be expressed with *Ken* or *Jo* and vice versa. But having said this, it should be noted that it is only through deep personal study that one will become aware of the spiritual relationship which is the true purpose of this vital *Riai* (sword, staff, and body). On these few pages we have chosen to focus on three fundamental applications in the following order: *Ken* to *Ken*, empty handed to *Ken*, and empty handed to *Jo*, demonstrating their basic interrelationship to the *Shiho-Nage* of this chapter.

AWASE - Blending with Ken

As *Uchi* (right) glides forward with overhead attack, *Uke* (left) moves to the left while retaining *Migi Hanmi* (right posture) and matches *Uchi's* cut, cutting to the top of *Uchi's Ken* (photos #1 #2 #3).

As *Uchi* raises *Ken* for second attack, *Uke* takes large gliding step with right foot, drawing *Ken* across front of *Uchi*. Stepping forward with left foot, *Uke* pivots back, matching *Uchi's* downward movement with a strike toward *Uchi's* head (photos #4 #5 #6).

TACHI-DORI *SWORD - TAKING*

1

Uke utilizes strike to side of neck/head from *Gyaku-Hanmi* (photo #1).

APPLIED PRINCIPLES: Stepping forward deeply, *Nage* blocks *Uke's* wrist area with left hand while driving sharp *Atemi* to temple, allowing arc of blade to complete swing harmlessly to the outside of *Nage's* new position (photos #2 #3).

2

3

4

5

6

7

8

9

Throwing left foot back, *Nage* grips handle of *Ken* with left hand while taking *Shiho-Nage* grip of *Uke's* right wrist with right hand (photo #4). Pivoting hips toward *Uke* while raising arms with strong *Kokyu* movement, *Nage* glides slightly forward with right foot (photo #5). Stepping through with left foot, *Nage* pivots hips powerfully clockwise and executes throw simultaneously relieving *Uke* of *Ken* and placing *Ken* tight to left hip, blade facing upward (photos #6 #7 #8 #9).

JO-DORI *STAFF - TAKING*

Uke utilizes thrusting attack from *Ai-Hanmi* (photo #1).

APPLIED PRINCIPLES: Obliquing hips, *Nage* glides forward and to the inside of thrust. Grasping *Jo* between *Uke's* grip with left hand and just forward of *Uke's* grip with right hand, *Nage* simultaneously draws hips back elongating *Uke's* thrust (photo #2).

Driving end of *Jo* under *Uke's* left arm, *Nage* lowers hips while raising arms and glides forward beneath *Uke's* outstretched arms (photo #3). Pivoting sharply clockwise while bringing *Jo* tight to left hip, *Nage* drives *Jo* deep to *Uke's* right rear corner to implement throw (photos #4 #5 #6).

NOTE: *Nage* must not allow *Jo* to be placed between *Uke* and *Nage*. Almost all weapon taking *Waza*, be they *Tanto*, *Jo*, or *Ken*, utilize the placement of *Nage's* body between *Uke* and his weapon.

KOTEGAESHI

(WRIST TURN)

Translated within the context of *Aikido* as "wrist turn," *Kotegaeshi* introduces both *Nage* and *Uke* to the accumulative effect of large spherical movements suddenly condensed to their nucleus, i.e. the outward rotation of *Uke's* wrist. The manipulative movements by *Nage* of *Uke's* wrist are described in the close-up section on the following page, but the successful application of this *Waza* (as with all in *Aikido*) lies in *Nage's* solidly grounded, fully connected, and powerfully engaged use of the hips as well as the power to be found deep within the *Seika-Tanden* (center). Extremely useful against a knife-wielding assailant, *Kotegaeshi*, upon first encounter, will seem to be relatively simple to master, but one will quickly discover the necessity of deep and lengthy exploration of the subtle qualities found within the dynamics of this explosive *Waza*.

NOTE: This page contains gripping, manipulation, and reinforcement application close-ups as they pertain to the *Waza* in this section.

APPLICATION: Securely grasp back of *Uke's* hand, being sure to take firm *Ken* grip with little finger, ring finger, and middle finger driven deeply into the palm around the base of *Uke's* thumb (photo to left).

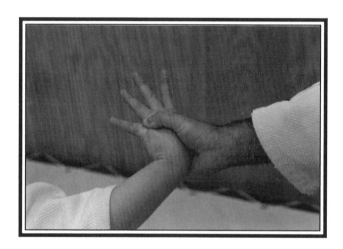

Turn *Uke's* wrist back on itself, driving his little finger over his wrist (this will save *Uke* from unnecessary cartilage damage). It is important that no air space be permitted between *Nage's* palm and the back of *Uke's* hand (photo center page).

Reinforce *Waza* with free hand by driving *Tegatana* (handblade) against gripping thumb (photo at right).

TSUKI KOTEGAESHI

1

Uke utilizes a thrusting attack from *Ai-Hanmi* (photo #1).

APPLIED PRINCIPLES: Driving forward and to the outside, *Nage* deflects attack (photo #2). Grasping *Uke's* wrist, *Nage* sweeps right foot back then left foot, draws *Uke* off balance and performs *Kotegaeshi* throw (photos #3 #4 #5).

2

3

4

5

7

6

Keeping *Kotegaeshi* grip, *Nage* steps to *Uke's* right side and controls elbow for turnover (photo #6). Throwing back right foot at a 45 degree angle to *Uke's* shoulder, *Nage* pins with standing *Katame Waza* (photo #7), see *Katame Waza* section.

TSUKI KOTEGAESHI *UCHI*

Uke utilizes a thrusting attack from *Ai-Hanmi* (photo #1).

APPLIED PRINCIPLES: *Nage* steps to the inside (live side) of thrust with right foot, while drawing left foot off attack line and meets *Uke's* arm at full extension (photo #2). Pushing arm down slightly, *Nage* shifts hips and steps to *Uke's* outside (photo #3).

Taking *Kotegaeshi* with left hand, *Nage* sweeps right foot back then left foot, drawing *Uke's* balance fully to rear (photos #4 #5).

CONTINUED

6

Throwing with sharp cut to *Uke's* right rear (photo #6), *Nage* keeps *Kotegaeshi* grip and takes elbow with right hand (photo #7).

7

8

Pressing elbow toward *Uke's* face, *Nage* turns *Uke* over with downward movement of hips while placing right knee at top of shoulder (photo #8). Pivoting left knee into *Uke's* armpit, *Nage* locks wrist and elbow to chest to implement *Katame Waza* (photo #9). See *Katame Waza* section (formal ending).

9

SHOMENUCHI KOTEGAESHI

Uke utilizes overhead strike from *Gyaku-Hanmi* (photo #1).

APPLIED PRINCIPLES: Stepping forward and to the outside of *Uke's* attack, *Nage* deflects with left forearm and takes control with right hand (photo #2). Throwing left foot back, *Nage* breaks *Uke's* balance making sure to move hands in relation to hips (photo #3).

Stepping back with right foot, *Nage* pivots hips sharply and applies *Kotegaeshi* with left hand reinforcement (photos #4 #5 #6).

NOTE: During *Atemi* application (photo #3) *Nage's* back must remain straight with controlling hand (hand holding *Uke's* wrist) kept in line with center.

YOKOMENUCHI KOTEGAESHI SOTO

1

Uke utilizes a side strike to head from *Ai-Hanmi* (photo #1).

APPLIED PRINCIPLES: As *Uke* steps forward with attack, *Nage* glides forcefully to the outside, stopping *Uke's* arm before it gains full momentum (photo #2), see *Yokomenuchi Sankyo* final note. Cutting behind *Uke*, *Nage* takes control by gripping arm from above with left hand, and aligning hips (photos #3 #4).

2

3

4

5

6

Throwing right foot back and applying *Atemi*, *Nage* draws *Uke* first into his center, then steps back with left foot and cuts sharply to *Uke's* right rear (photos #5 #6).

YOKOMENUCHI KOTEGAESHI

Uke utilizes a side strike to head from *Ai-Hanmi* (photo #1).

APPLIED PRINCIPLES: Stepping forward and to the inside of *Uke*, *Nage* deflects attacking hand out and down with right forearm, while applying *Atemi* with left hand (photo #2).

Taking attacking hand from beneath with left hand, *Nage* steps back with right foot and completes *Hanmi* change (photo #3).

NOTE: *Uke* has been brought past original point of focus and balance has been broken.

OBSERVATION: Triangle *N* faces triangle *U* (photo #1), triangle *N & U* meet and form square (photo #2), triangle *N* separates and dominates centerline (photo #3).

Stepping in with right foot and pivoting hips while changing grip to right hand, *Nage* applies *Atemi* to the left side of *Uke's* head (photo #4).

NOTE: All hand changes should be positive, i.e. one hand grips fully before the other relinquishes its hold. Although this *Waza* may be done with cutting or fencing type handwork up until point of *Kotegaeshi*, this is not a *Kihon* (basic) application nor does it promote full solid control of *Uke*.

Throwing left foot back, *Nage* draws *Uke* around, keeping hands in relation to center (photo #5). Stepping forward with left foot and retreating right (photo #6), *Nage* then reinforces *Kotegaeshi* hold with left hand and cuts authoritatively to *Uke's* left rear (photo #7).

NOTE: Final execution of *Kotegaeshi* may be performed in a number of ways: first, by cutting sharply while performing a strong pivot; second, by using advancing-retreating footwork; third, by cutting while performing a *Tenkan* turning movement.

OBSERVATION: If neutral with *Uke*, pivot and cut sharply. If pulled by *Uke* weight, advance and cut powerfully. If pushed by *Uke's* weight, *Tenkan* and cut fully.

RYOTETORI KOTEGAESHI

Uke utilizes two wrist grab (one on one) from *Gyaku-Hanmi* (photo #1).

APPLIED PRINCIPLES: Gliding to outside with a forceful counterclockwise rotation of hips, *Nage* draws left hand over right and breaks *Uke's* grip (photo #2 & close-up).

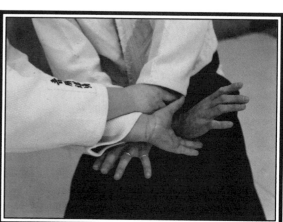

Bringing freed right hand back over *Uke's* left wrist, *Nage* takes *Kotegaeshi*. Stepping back first with left foot, then with right (photos #3 #4), *Nage* cuts sharply to *Uke's* left rear, applying in this instance *Kotegaeshi* in a *Nage Waza* (throwing technique) form (photo #5).

OBSERVATION: Free yourself from the want/need to down your partner. Fill yourself with the power of correct *Kiri-No-Ken* (repetitious cutting with heavy wooden sword performed on *Tanren-Uchi*) when applying *Kotegaeshi Waza*.

USHIRO HIJITORI KOTEGAESHI

1

Uke utilizes two elbow grab from rear (photo #1).

APPLIED PRINCIPLES: Immediately *Nage* drops and drives center back into *Uke* while forming a powerful circle with arms. Sliding back and underneath *Uke's* elbow, *Nage* draws *Uke* forward and takes *Kotegaeshi* with left hand's thumb pointing down (photo #2).

2

3

4

Lifting up and cutting *Uke's* grip from sleeve (photo #3), *Nage* cuts sharply to *Uke's* right rear executing *Kotegaeshi* projection (photos #4 #5).

NOTE: From this position *Nage* may apply any number of endings (see *Katame Waza* section for *Kihon* and *Oyo-Katame*).

5

KAITEN-NAGE

(ROTARY THROW)

Translated within the context of *Aikido* as "rotary throw," *Kaiten-Nage* refers to the powerful circular motion applied to *Uke's* straightened arm as it is driven above and behind the back while simultaneously suppressing the head downward, creating an axis for the projection of *Uke's* body. From large free-flowing rolls to tight bone-jarring tailbone landings, *Kaiten-Nage* freely crosses the spectrum in its application, making it yet another vital tool of development for *Uke* as well as *Nage*. Manifested as a hard triangle encased within a soft circle, *Kaiten-Nage* presents itself as a formidable study in the nature and application of the principles of *In* and *Yo*. Needless to say *Kaiten-Nage* demands lengthy and introspective effort.

KATATETORI KAITEN-NAGE UCHI

Uke utilizes straight hand grab from *Gyaku-Hanmi* (photo #1).

APPLIED PRINCIPLES: Gliding in and to the outside of *Uke's* forward foot, *Nage* cuts both arms upward with *Kokyu* and applies *Atemi* to face (photo #2). Stepping forward with left foot under *Uke's* arm, *Nage* pivots sharply back to control center (photo #3).

Simultaneously drawing right foot back and cutting down with arm, driving *Uke* forward and off balance, *Nage* suppresses *Uke's* head and positions arm over back (photo #4). Extending right arm fully, *Nage* drives right hip forward and steps in projecting *Uke's* arm toward and between his head and shoulder area executing *Nage Waza* (photos #5 #6).

KATATETORI KAITEN-NAGE *SOTO*

Uke utilizes straight hand grab from *Gyaku-Hanmi* (photo #1).

APPLIED PRINCIPLES: Driving right arm up and to the outside with strong *Kokyu* movement, *Nage* rotates *Tegatana* to the little finger side of *Uke's* wrist and applies *Atemi* to ribs with left hand (photo #2).

Cutting *Uke's* arm down, *Nage* glides back drawing *Uke* forward and off balance (photo #3). Suppressing head with left hand, *Nage* rotates arm above and behind *Uke's* back (photo #4). Extending right arm fully, *Nage* drives right hip forward and steps in projecting *Uke's* arm toward and between his head and right shoulder area (photo #5) executing *Nage Waza* (throwing technique).

TSUKI KAITEN-NAGE

1

Uke utilizes thrusting attack from *Ai-Hanmi* (photo #1).

APPLIED PRINCIPLES: Gliding powerfully forward and to the outside, *Nage* pivots hips to align with *Uke* while simultaneously deflecting attack (photo #2).

2

NOTE: *Nage's* forearm to elbow placement eliminates countering by *Uke* with elbow or back-fist strike (photo #2).

3

4

5

Sliding hips back, *Nage* drives arm down, back, and over *Uke*, suppressing head with right hand (photo #3). Extending left arm fully, *Nage* rotates left hip forward and steps in projecting *Uke's* arm outward between opposite side of head and shoulder for *Nage Waza* (photos #4 #5).

NOTE: *Nage* may apply *Atemi* with left knee to *Uke's* face (photo #3); this is executed by drawing *Uke's* head back as *Nage* rotates left hip forward so as not to lose control/balance.

USHIRO RYOTETORI KAITEN-NAGE

1

Uke utilizes two rear wrist grab (photo #1).

APPLIED PRINCIPLES: Raising both arms with strong *Kokyu* power while keeping arms close to body (causing *Uke's* elbows to remain outside), *Nage* glides back and under *Uke's* left arm (photo #2). See observation *Ushiro Ryokatatori Ikkyo Irimi*. Cutting right hand over *Uke's* left forearm, *Nage* frees left wrist (photo #3).

2

3

Suppressing *Uke's* head with left hand, *Nage* rotates arm above and behind back (photo #4). Extending right arm fully, *Nage* drives forward with hip, steps in and executes *Nage Waza* (photo #5).

4

NOTE: *Nage* should align center keeping *Uke's* balance, arm may then be projected between opposite side of head and shoulder area. Sequence of throw: arm extended, hip engaged, and only then does *Nage* step forward.

OBSERVATION: Throw as though thrusting with *Ken*, i.e. hip, hand, and right foot powerfully thrust forward from *Hidari-Hanmi* (left posture), or vice-versa.

5

YOKOMENUCHI KAITEN-NAGE *TENKAN/URA*

Uke utilizes a side strike to the head from *Ai-Hanmi* (photo #1).

APPLIED PRINCIPLES: Stepping forward and to the inside of *Uke's* attack, *Nage* deflects strike out and downward with right forearm while applying *Atemi* toward *Uke's* face with left hand (photo #2).

NOTE: As in observation for *Yokomenuchi Shiho-Nage* (see *Shiho-Nage* section), it is very important to disrupt *Uke's* balance by first disturbing then taking control of *Uke's Chushin* (centerline) of attack.

Continuing to deflect attack downward, *Nage* controls *Uke's* arm by gripping wrist with left hand while directing arm past centerline, breaking *Uke's* balance circularly forward (photo #3).

NOTE: *Nage* must be sure to direct arm past center, allowing a forward step directly toward *Uke* without the necessity to step around arm. *Uke's* left shoulder can be suppressed, breaking *Uke's* balance by rotating *Uke's* wrist so that little finger side of hand is up with arm held straight (photo #3).

4

Stepping forward with right foot, *Nage* drives *Uke's* arm down with right hand while moving left hand to suppress *Uke's* head (photo #4). Sliding farther past *Uke's* side while rotating hips counterclockwise, *Nage* drives *Uke's* arm up and over back (photo #5).

5

6

7

8

Throwing left foot back 45 degrees, *Nage* draws *Uke's* head in and down while driving arm farther over back, causing *Uke's* balance to be broken fully to the outside of his right hip (photo #6). Extending right arm fully, *Nage* rotates right hip forward, implementing throw (photo #7). Stepping forward with right foot (photo #8), *Nage* expends force of hip rotation and executes *Zanshin* (lingering connecting spirit).

KOSHI-NAGE

(HIP THROW)

Literally translated as "hip throw," *Koshi-Nage* refers to the projection of *Uke* over the area of *Nage's* hips at the rear pelvic region. At first glance *Koshi-Nage* may appear to be lifting, loading, and finally tossing *Uke* to the mat, but this is by no means the case. *Koshi-Nage* is the art of threading the hips beneath *Uke's* center of gravity, thus bringing about a natural orbital motion of *Uke's* entire body. Done correctly, *Koshi-Nage* is an expression of connection at its highest level, free-floating form without form, power without violence. Needless to say, the necessity for the proper development of an advanced level of *Ukemi* (art of receiving), is a prerequisite for the addition of *Koshi-Nage* to daily training. A helpful hint as you progress is to look forward to your practice of *Koshi-Nage* and prepare to guide your mind through the outward process, while releasing your body to the overall experience.

SHOMENUCHI KOSHI-NAGE

1

2

3

APPLIED PRINCIPLES: Taking the initiative, *Nage* glides forward in left *Hanmi* while driving *Tegatana* (handblade) toward *Uke's* face, causing *Uke* to reflect (*Suigetsu*-moon on water) *Nage's* motion (photos #1 #2). Stepping in with right foot while obliquing hips, *Nage* drives right *Atemi* to *Uke's* ribcage (photo #3).

4

Shifting left foot back to 45 degree angle, *Nage* reaches up with right hand taking *Sankyo* type *Ken* grip (palm on top/back of hand) and guides *Uke's* arm down and to outside (photo #4). Lifting arm and rotating wrist counterclockwise toward *Uke*, *Nage* drives forward with left *Atemi* while positioning left foot between *Uke's* legs (photo #5).

5

6

Throwing right foot back 180 degrees in front of *Uke*, *Nage* continues rotation of wrist as it passes overhead. Keeping strong extension up and outward with right hand, *Nage* lowers and fully engages hips (photo #6). Taking *Uke's* balance from below his center of gravity, *Nage* throws with a smooth arc over hips (photos #7 #8).

7

NOTE: As in all *Koshi-Nage*, *Nage* must take care to strongly shift weight and hips from *Uke's* initial side to point of landing during arc of throw. This shifting action not only creates a more positive projection and strong hip development, but also is of utmost importance to protect against the possibility of *Uke* landing on the outside of *Nage's* leg. The fear of this kind of injury is most likely the basis for the propagation of most *Judo* type *Hana Koshi-Nage* (popping/recoiling) seen in many styles of *Aikido* today. See notation *Ryokatatori Koshi-Nage*.

8

YOKOMENUCHI KOSHI-NAGE

1

Uke utilizes a side strike to the head from *Ai-Hanmi* (photo #1).

APPLIED PRINCIPLES: Responding with inside entry, *Nage* takes *Uke's* right wrist in *Shiho-Nage* type *Ken* grip (photos #2 #3), see *Yokomenuchi Shiho-Nage Irimi* for entry.

2

3

4

5

6

Stepping to *Uke's* right side, *Nage* aligns left foot with the outside of *Uke's* right foot while lowering and fully engaging hips below *Uke's* center (photo #4). *Nage* throws by arcing *Uke* over hips in one smooth motion (photos #5 #6).

USHIRO RYOTETORI KOSHI-NAGE

1

Uke utilizes a two rear wrist hold from *Ai-Hanmi* (photo #1).

APPLIED PRINCIPLES: Using strong *Kokyu* power, *Nage* raises both arms in front of forehead and takes *Uke's* left wrist in *Sankyo* type *Ken* grip with right hand (photo #2). Keeping right arm extended up and outward, *Nage* rotates upper torso out and under *Uke's* left arm. Maintaining alignment, *Nage* lowers and fully engages hips below *Uke's* center (photo #3).

2

3

4

Having fully engaged *Uke*, *Nage* throws in one smooth arcing motion (photos #4 #5).

NOTE: *Nage* has the option of hooking *Uke's* lower leg with free hand during many *Koshi-Nage* (as shown above); however, it should be closely noted that *Nage* should never lift *Uke's* leg, instead hand is used to assist the momentum created by *Nage's* hips slipping beneath *Uke's* center.

5

RYOTETORI KOSHI-NAGE

1

Uke utilizes two wrist grab from *Ai-Hanmi* (photo #1).

APPLIED PRINCIPLES: Stepping in and to the outside with right foot, *Nage* sharply obliques hips while driving left forearm up under right with strong *Kokyu* power (photo #2), see close-up *Ryotetori Irimi-Nage*.

2

3

4

5

Lowering hips, *Nage* steps under and in front of *Uke* with right foot and places left foot back between *Uke's* legs. Extending right arm upward, *Nage* locks *Uke's* left wrist over right (photo #3). *Nage* fully engages both hips below *Uke's* center and throws with smooth arc over hips (photos #4 #5).

NOTE: As in all *Koshi-Nage*, *Nage* looks up during hip engagement; this will assist in the insurance of the proper engagement of both hips and not just the inside (closest to *Uke*).

KATATORI SHOMENUCHI KOSHI-NAGE

Uke utilizes a one lapel or shoulder grab and a downward strike to head from *Gyaku-Hanmi* (photos #1 #2).

APPLIED PRINCIPLES: Placing right foot to the inside at a 90 degree angle while driving right arm up to *Uke's* left elbow with strong *Kokyu* power, *Nage* positions *Uke's* elbow over *Uke's* center by shifting hips forcefully (photo #3).

Sliding right hand up *Uke's* arm, *Nage* takes *Ken* grip (palm to pulse side of wrist with thumb pointing down) and steps through and in front of *Uke* with right foot while lowering hips (photo #4). Fully engaging both hips below *Uke's* center of gravity, *Nage* completes throw with smooth arcing motion while shifting weight from left to right foot (photos #5 #6).

RYOKATATORI KOSHI-NAGE

1

2

3

PRE-NOTE: The linking essence of *Koshi-Nage* to all *Waza* is felt in one instance through the necessity of a strong stable hip foundation. As the distance between *Nage* and *Uke* increases, it is of utmost importance to maintain this hip relationship, for while not physically contacting your partner with your hips, the essential spirit of engagement must be constant. One example of this interrelationship may be found on this and the next page, explored through related forms of *Koshi* and *Kokyu-Nage*.

Uke utilizes a two lapel grab from *Ai-Hanmi* (photo #1).

APPLIED PRINCIPLES: Stepping forward with right foot while obliquing hips, *Nage* drives *Atemi* up and between *Uke's* arms to face (photo #2). Extending right arm upward, *Nage* positions left foot back between *Uke's* legs, while lowering and fully engaging hips below *Uke's* center (photo #3). *Nage* throws by arcing *Uke* over hips in one smooth motion (photos #4 #5).

4

5

NOTE: To develop hip power and stability within *Koshi-Nage*, it should be noted that *Nage* does not pull in right foot nor pop hips during throw (photos #3 #4 #5). *Koshi-Nage* performed with pulling and/or popping movements are forms of *Hane-Koshi* and should be considered *Oyo* not *Kihon Waza* (varied not basic technique) within *Aikido*.

RYOKATATORI KOKYU-NAGE

1

2

3

4

Uke utilizes a two lapel grab from *Ai-Hanmi* (photo #1).

APPLIED PRINCIPLES: Driving *Atemi* between arms to *Uke's* face with right hand, *Nage* places right foot toe to toe with *Uke's* left foot (photo #2). Aligning left foot at *Uke's* side, *Nage* engages right forearm with inside of *Uke's* right elbow (photo #3). With driving cut from hips, *Nage* throws to *Uke's* right front corner (photos #4 #5).

5

TENCHI-NAGE

(HEAVEN - EARTH THROW)

Literally translated as "heaven-earth throw," *Tenchi-Nage* refers to the projection of *Uke* brought about by *Nage* entering deeply into *Uke's* posture while simultaneously expanding upward and downward. Enveloped in the vortex of this movement, *Uke* is compellingly projected to the rear as *Nage* binds the two forces together at the center.

> Dreaming of the Heavens
>
> We work the soil with our hands
>
> Truly man is the Center
>
> of *In-Yo* within his Universe

Within the above short poem lies the essence of *Tenchi-Nage*. If we are diligent in our endeavor, *Tenchi-Nage* can help to lead us to understand, through the dynamics of its nature, that though we carry heaven within our heads and earth under our feet, it is within our heart/soul/center that is placed the realization of right and wrong, good and bad, superiority or inferiority, and the power of choosing and following the correct or incorrect path. Intriguingly simple while at the same time complex and perplexing, *Tenchi-Nage* deserves lengthy exploration.

RYOTETORI TENCHI-NAGE

Uke utilizes two wrist grab from *Gyaku-Hanmi* (photo #1).

APPLIED PRINCIPLES: Gliding deeply to the outside while driving *Uke's* right hand behind and below center, *Nage* breaks *Uke's* balance to side and downward. *Nage* simultaneously raises *Uke* up from center with *Tegatana* (handblade) placed inside of grip and draws right foot off line (photo #2).

Stepping deeply behind *Uke* with right foot, *Nage* drives right hand over and behind shoulder, breaking *Uke's* balance fully for throw (photos #3 #4).

NOTE: The above inset photo shows the angle and depth of entry which *Nage* must employ during the execution of *Tenchi-Nage*.

OBSERVATION: In one instant *Nage* should give *Uke* the feeling of being enveloped within and drawn to the center of a great circular sphere, and at the very next instant expelled outward as if magnetically repulsed by the very object of attraction.

RYOTETORI TENCHI-NAGE *TENKAN/URA*

1

Uke utilizes two wrist grab from *Gyaku-Hanmi* (photo #1).

APPLIED PRINCIPLES: Bringing left *Tegatana* to inside of *Uke's* wrist, *Nage* glides powerfully to the outside, forming a central axis with right hand and foot placed behind and below *Uke's* center (photo #2).

2

Throwing left foot back with strong *Tenkan* motion, *Nage* simultaneously drives left *Tegatana* up and into *Uke's* wrist while drawing with strong hip rotation (photo #3). Stepping deeply behind with left foot as *Uke's* center passes, *Nage* drives left hand behind *Uke* for throw (photos #4 #5).

3

4

NOTE: To generate full power within *Tenchi-Nage*, it should be noted that as *Nage* raises the upper body, there must be a simultaneous lowering of the hips.

OBSERVATION: It may be said that *Tenchi-Nage* (heaven and earth throw) does not receive its name solely from one hand reaching upward and the other down, but also from the upper body's expansion upward and the lower body's drive downward, commonly bound by the *Tanden* (center).

5

RYOTETORI TENCHI-NAGE GYAKU WAZA

1

Uke utilizes a two wrist grab from *Ai-Hanmi* (photo #1).

APPLIED PRINCIPLES: Gliding forward to *Uke's* left side, *Nage* drives right hand below *Uke's* center while raising left hand upward to the inside of *Uke's* right wrist (photo #2).

2

3

NOTE: This application of *Tenchi-Nage* may also be termed as *Tenchi* to *Kokyu-Nage Henka Waza*, in that the initial *Tenchi* movement is aborted and then followed immediately by a throw in the opposite direction. Having said this, it should be noted that the properties of lowering the hips while raising the arm, inherent in *Tenchi-Nage* is a must to the proper execution of this *Waza*, therefore *Tenchi-Nage Gyaku* (opposite) *Waza* is also a viable definition.

4

Rotating hips powerfully counterclockwise, *Nage* cuts down and over *Uke's* wrist with left hand while driving right *Tegatana* up *Uke's* left forearm to elbow (photo #3). Continuing hip rotation, *Nage* directs *Uke's* balance over and behind right shoulder, executing throw (photos #4 #5).

NOTE: It is important to apply this reversal only in certain situations: one, *Nage* moves directly to *Uke's* live side (*Uke* in right *Hanmi*, *Nage* moves to *Uke's* left, photo #2); two, *Uke* steps back during *Nage's* advance, creating a live side entry. If *Nage* attempts this reversal from *Uke's* dead side (same side as *Uke's Hanmi*), it will allow *Uke* to step forward regaining balance.

5

AIKI-OTOSHI
(AIKI DROP)

SUMI-OTOSHI
(CORNER DROP)

AIKI-NAGE
(AIKI THROW)

The first portion of this section deals with *Aiki-Otoshi*, translated from Japanese as *Ai* = harmony, *Ki* = energy/life-force/spirit, *Otoshi* = drop, *Aiki-Otoshi* brings us once again into full physical connection with *Uke*. As with *Koshi-Nage*, *Aiki-Otoshi* must not be a form of exertive lifting but instead a joining so complete as to bring about the irresistible ascension of *Uke's* body, free from unnecessary power confrontation. The second and third portions covered in this section touch on applications of *Sumi-Otoshi* (corner drop) and *Aiki-Nage* (harmonized energy throw). Both deal with joining the inertia generated by *Uke's* attack to bring about the projection of *Uke* with only minimal physical contact, yet at the same time these two *Waza* are fully charged with the concepts of engagement without confrontation which are so necessary to the execution of *Aiki-Otoshi*. The essence of this paradox of connection with and without contact asks us to deal with our training on many more levels than we will at first perceive. Needless to say, *Aiki-Otoshi*, *Sumi-Otoshi*, and *Aiki-Nage* call for and should receive extensive study.

USHIRO RYOKATATORI AIKI-OTOSHI

Uke utilizes two rear shoulder grab (photo #1).

APPLIED PRINCIPLES: Moving to the left, *Nage* creates an opening between *Uke's* left hip and *Nage's* right. Energizing upper body with *Kokyu*, *Nage* drives arms outward, forming an open ring (photo #2). Stepping behind *Uke* with right foot, *Nage* suddenly lowers hips and closes arms around *Uke's* legs, just behind knees (photo #3).

NOTE: *Nage* must keep back straight, hips below *Uke's*, and abdomen tight.

Driving hips forward and under *Uke's* center, *Nage* scoops legs at bend in knees. Keeping full hip engagement, *Nage* rotates hips clockwise, pivoting into a right *Hanmi* while throwing *Uke* to rear (photos #4 #5).

NOTE: *Nage* uses full hip engagement to both lift and throw; arms should be used only to guide and direct *Uke's* fall.

180

YOKOMENUCHI AIKI-OTOSHI

Uke utilizes strike to side of head from *Ai-Hanmi* (photo #1).

APPLIED PRINCIPLES: *Nage* responds with blending entry to the inside (photos #2 #3). See *Yokomenuchi Shiho-Nage*.

Applying a strong clockwise rotation to *Uke's* wrist, *Nage* lifts arm and thrusts upper body beneath it (photo #4). Throwing *Uke's* arm over back, *Nage* steps behind and directly into center with right foot while applying *Atemi* with right elbow (photo #5). Lowering and fully engaging hips, *Nage* encircles *Uke's* knees (photo #6). Driving hips under *Uke's* center, *Nage* scoops legs at bend in knees. Maintaining full hip engagement, *Nage* pivots into a right *Hanmi* while throwing *Uke* to rear (photo #7).

RYOKATATORI AIKI-OTOSHI OYO WAZA

1

Uke utilizes two lapel/shoulder grab from *Ai-Hanmi* (photo #1).

APPLIED PRINCIPLES: Stepping directly back with right foot, *Nage* drives *Atemi* upward between *Uke's* arms and toward face (photo #2). Bringing right arm over and cutting downward with forearm to inside of *Uke's* left elbow, *Nage* drives up and outward with left forearm, creating a circular opening in *Uke's* arms (photo #3).

2

Inserting upper body under *Uke's* right arm, *Nage* simultaneously steps forward and to the outside of *Uke's* left leg (photo #4). Placing right elbow in the small of *Uke's* back, *Nage* reaches around *Uke's* hips while sweeping *Uke's* inner right knee with left hand. Positioning *Uke's* shoulder to the outside and behind *Nage's* right hip, *Nage* drives hips beneath *Uke's* center while rotating hips clockwise, lifting *Uke* to execute throw (photos #5 #6 #7). See note *Ushiro Ryokatatori Aiki-Otoshi*.

3

4

5

6

OBSERVATION: *Uke's* loss of balance will create a desire (within the physical body) to fall forward over the left shoulder (photos #3 #4). *Nage* must not be an obstacle, but instead a catalyst for the completion of this desire.

NOTE: This *Waza* may also be performed as a *Kokyu-Nage* by driving shoulder and right arm upward beneath *Uke's* right arm while pivoting hips toward *Uke* as described in *Otoshi* text. See *Ushiro Ryokatatori Kokyu-Nage* (*Kokyu-Nage* section).

7

KATATETORI SUMI-OTOSHI

1

Uke utilizes straight hand grab from *Gyaku-Hanmi* (photo #1).

APPLIED PRINCIPLES: Gliding forward while rotating hips clockwise, *Nage* aligns with and collects *Uke's* energy (photo #2). Throwing right leg back 180 degrees, *Nage* draws *Uke's* balance around (photo #3).

2

3

4

5

6

Gliding sharply forward and behind *Uke's* right rear corner, *Nage* leads *Uke's* arm deeply to rear while lowering to right knee (photo #4). Cutting downward with left hand and simultaneously cutting upward against *Uke's* right lower calf, *Nage* executes *Sumi-Otoshi* (corner drop).

YOKOMENUCHI AIKI-NAGE

1

Uke utilizes a side strike to the head from *Ai-Hanmi* (photo #1).

APPLIED PRINCIPLES: As *Uke* steps forward committing to a powerful strike, *Nage* glides deeply forward, placing left foot in front of *Uke's* right foot while lowering torso and hips (photo #2).

2

Sliding down onto left knee, *Nage* begins to move beneath *Uke's* center of gravity (photo #3). Rotating hips while drawing in right knee, *Nage* passes completely beneath *Uke's* center and into *Uke's* original position, turning to and aligning with *Uke's* direction of fall (photos #4 #5).

3

4

NOTE: The inherent danger of this *Waza* comes when *Uke* attempts to hold his ground or to dive over *Nage*; both actions may result in serious injury to *Uke*. Taking care not to plant feet firmly and responding by rolling off *Nage's* back is *Uke's* proper avenue of defense. Full commitment to the attack and a heightened sense and understanding of *Ukemi* is necessary for the correct and safe practice of this *Waza*.

5

JUJI-GARAMI

(CROSS ENTWINING TECHNIQUE)

Literally translated as "cross entwining," *Juji-Garami* refers to technique in which *Nage* entangles *Uke's* arms to execute a throw or to pin *Uke* to the mat. Sometimes referred to as *Juji-Nage* (cross throw), *Juji-Garami* was originally developed as a means to dislocate and/or break an attacker's arms, thus rendering him helpless. Applied within the framework of *Aikido*, we are asked to employ this potentially dangerous *Waza* in a safe yet robust manner, controlling *Uke* fully while at the same time (as with all *Aikido Waza*) using only the amount of severity warranted. *Juji-Garami* demands that we entwine not only *Uke's* arms but also our mind, body and spirit with that of *Uke* to bring about an outcome which is mutually advantageous, i.e. *Nage* fully controls both his own as well as *Uke's* aggressive actions while *Uke*, though completely caught up on the receiving end of the *Waza*, remains free from unnecessary harm. Extended hours of training are required on the long road to absorbing the significance of this explosive *Waza*.

USHIRO RYOTETORI JUJI-GARAMI

1

Uke utilizes two rear wrist grab (photo #1).

APPLIED PRINCIPLES: Using strong *Kokyu* power, *Nage* raises both arms keeping *Uke's* elbows to outside. *Nage* then glides back and under *Uke's* left arm breaking *Uke's* balance forward (photo #2). Taking *Uke's* wrists (see note, center page), *Nage* drives right foot forward in front of *Uke* while entwining *Uke's* arms (photo #3).

2

NOTE: High hand should be positioned so that palm faces toward *Uke* with thumb pointing toward the thumb of *Uke's* grip. Low hand should be positioned so that palm faces toward *Uke* with thumb pointing toward little finger side of *Uke's* grip (photo #2).

3

4

Cutting vigorously to point just inside of forward foot, *Nage* executes throw (photos #4 #5).

NOTE: *Nage* must solidly entwine *Uke's* arms at elbows, following natural bend of elbow. Allowing *Uke's* high arm to straighten may result in severe damage to elbow.

5

KATATORI JUJI-GARAMI *OYO-KOSHI WAZA*

Uke utilizes one lapel/shoulder grab from *Gyaku-Hanmi* (photo #1).

APPLIED PRINCIPLES: Offsetting right foot at 90 degree angle, *Nage* drives *Tegatana* toward *Uke's* face causing *Uke* to block (photo #2). Peeling grip from lapel with right hand, *Nage* takes *Uke's* wrists and steps forward into center (photo #3). See *Ushiro Ryotetori Juji-Garami* for hold.

Lowering and engaging hips fully (photo #4), *Nage* executes *Oyo-Koshi Waza* (photos #5 #6). See *Koshi-Nage* section. Trapping right wrist at shoulder, *Nage* turns *Uke* over with clockwise rotation applying pressure at inner elbow and pins *Uke* to mat (photos #7 #8). See *Katame Waza* section.

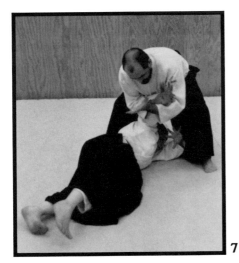

RYOTEMOCHI JUJI-GARAMI

Uke utilizes a two hands on one wrist hold from *Gyaku-Hanmi* (photo #1).

NOTE: In *Ryotemochi* (*Morotetori*), *Uke* should position outside hand higher on arm to secure strongest grip. This enables *Uke* to control *Nage* with a push/pull movement if *Nage* attempts a strike or kick toward *Uke*.

APPLIED PRINCIPLES: Gliding forward and to the outside while pivoting hips to align with *Uke's* direction, *Nage* lowers shoulder, elbow, and hips in one motion, causing *Uke* to lose balance forward (photo #2).

NOTE: *Nage's* held arm should be at a 45 degree angle with elbow positioned closer to *Uke* than wrist. Otherwise *Uke* can again utilize a push/pull countering movement.

Throwing left leg back 180 degrees while drawing *Uke's* balance forward and around, *Nage* positions *Uke* so that *Uke's* weight is on inside forward foot (photo #3).

Taking *Uke's* right wrist with held hand, *Nage* peels *Uke's* left grip free and fully entwines arms (photo #4). See *Ushiro Ryotetori Juji-Garami* for proper grip positioning.

5

6

Driving forward with strong hip rotation, *Nage* cuts to point just inside of forward foot (photo #5). *Nage* maintains a firm grip on *Uke's* inside hand (left) to control positioning of fall (photo #6).

7

NOTE: To apply *Katame Waza*, *Nage* must maintain a secure *Ken* grip with elbow slightly bent and hips firmly planted, not allowing weight to shift forward over *Uke*.

Taking *Uke's* left hand in *Kotegaeshi* grip with right hand, *Nage* moves left hand to *Uke's* elbow while stepping to far side of *Uke* with right foot (photo #7). Directing *Uke's* elbow toward mat, *Nage* rotates hips and draws left foot in, fully turning *Uke*. Assuming *Seiza* straddling *Uke's* shoulder, *Nage* applies pin (photo #8). See *Katame Waza* section.

8

IRIMI-NAGE

(ENTERING THROW)

Translated within the context of *Aikido* as "entering throw," *Irimi-Nage* refers to technique in which *Nage* enters, seemingly, directly into *Uke's* posture to take control of the dead spot at *Uke's* back. *Irimi-Nage* may be performed in a soft forgiving manner or as the disciplined explosion of positive energy, giving us realistic insight into the prospect that front and rear, left and right could just possibly be the same direction. *Irimi-Nage* presents us with a medium in which to begin to understand the straight line as a circle while simultaneously perceiving the circle which exists within the line. *O'Sensei* has been quoted on many occasions as having referred to *Irimi-Nage* as the twenty-year technique. Keeping this in mind we must attempt to cut to the heart of our training with each application, striving daily to propel ourselves toward a fuller understanding of this powerful *Waza*.

SHOMENUCHI IRIMI-NAGE *SIDE VIEW*

Uke utilizes overhead strike stepping forward from *Gyaku-Hanmi* (photo #1).

APPLIED PRINCIPLES: Gliding forward, *Nage* deflects strike with right forearm, then steps behind *Uke* with left foot and aligns hips with direction of attack (photos #2 #3).

Grasping *Uke's* collar at nape of neck, *Nage* draws *Uke's* head sharply to right shoulder while throwing right foot back 180 degrees (photos #4 #5). As *Uke's* hips pass *Nage's* center, *Nage* drives right arm forward and steps deeply behind *Uke* with right foot for throw (photo #6) see front view next page.

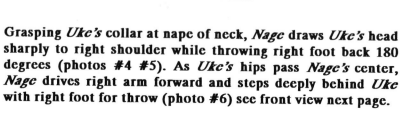

194

SHOMENUCHI IRIMI-NAGE *FRONT VIEW*

Front view picks up with *Nage* aligned at *Uke's* side (photo #1). Throwing back right foot, *Nage* draws *Uke* around (photos #2 #3).

NOTE: Relationship of *Uke's* head and *Nage's* hip must stay constant.

1

2

3

4

Keeping head pinned at the shoulder as *Uke's* center passes, *Nage* first drives right arm up and over *Uke* (photo #4), then steps deeply behind *Uke* with the right foot, physically taking the mutual center to implement throw (photos #5 #6).

5

6

NOTE: Throughout this *Waza*, but especially emphasized at the end, *Nage* must maintain a feeling of screwing his hips into the ground.

SHOMENUCHI IRIMI-NAGE *SUIGETSU WAZA*

1

APPLIED PRINCIPLES: Taking the initiative, *Nage* glides forward driving *Tegatana* (handblade) toward *Uke's* face. *Uke* responds by stepping forward to block with right arm, reflecting *Nage's* motion (photos #1 #2).

2

3

At the instant of contact, *Nage* opens hips to the outside while stepping forward with left foot to align with *Uke* (photo #3). Drawing head to shoulder while gliding slightly deeper, *Nage* pivots hips sharply toward *Uke* (photo #4). Driving right arm up and over *Uke*, *Nage* steps fully behind and executes throw (photos #5 #6). See *Tsuki Irimi-Nage*.

TSUKI IRIMI-NAGE

1

2

3

Uke utilizes a mid-level thrusting strike from *Ai-Hanmi* (photo #1).

APPLIED PRINCIPLES: Gliding forward and to the outside, *Nage* obliques and opens hips to allow strike to pass while aligning stance with *Uke's* line of attack (photo #2).

NOTE: *Nage* firmly grasps *Uke's* collar at nape of neck and draws head toward left shoulder. It is important when *Irimi-Nage* is performed rigorously that *Nage* utilizes this type of grip rather then gripping the neck itself, as this may lead to serious injury to *Uke*.

4

Pivoting hips powerfully towards *Uke*, *Nage* glides deeper behind *Uke* while encircling *Uke's* head with left arm. *Nage* draws *Uke's* weight to his inside foot, breaking *Uke's* balance to rear (photo #3). Stepping deeply behind *Uke*, *Nage* executes throw (photos #4 #5).

OBSERVATION: *Nage* seeks to create a bond with *Uke*, such as dirt to the farmers hands, only to be washed off by a crisp clean technique.

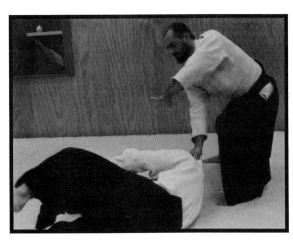

5

RYOTETORI IRIMI-NAGE

1

2

3

4

Uke utilizes two wrist grab from *Ai-Hanmi* (photo #1).

APPLIED PRINCIPLES: Powerfully rotating hips counterclockwise while raising arms (left under right) with strong *Kokyu* movement, *Nage* glides forward and to the outside trapping *Uke's* left arm, simultaneously *Nage* frees right wrist from grip (photo #2). See close-up photo below. Aligning postures, *Nage* takes *Uke's* collar with right hand, slightly offsets left foot, and draws head to shoulder (photo #3). Pivoting hips toward *Uke*, *Nage* leads first with arm, then steps deeply behind to execute throw (photos #4 #5 #6). See *Tsuki Irimi-Nage*.

5

Directing right thumb toward thumb and index finger of *Uke's* grip, *Nage* breaks hold with powerful hip rotation away from *Uke* (close-up below).

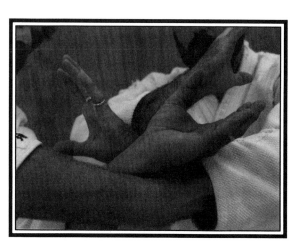

6

KATATETORI IRIMI-NAGE *OYO WAZA*

1

3

Uke utilizes straight hand grab from *Gyaku-Hanmi* (photo #1).

APPLIED PRINCIPLES: Gliding forward and to the outside, *Nage* wraps *Uke's* arm back to shoulder (photo #2).

2

4

5

Drawing *Uke* in and tight to body, *Nage* extends left arm over and behind *Uke* (photo #3). Stepping deeply behind *Uke's* center, *Nage* drives forward lowering and rotating hips to execute throw (photos #4 #5 #6).

NOTE: This *Oyo Waza* of *Irimi-Nage* is done from a very low hip position and great care should be taken to keep *Uke's* body tight during throw.

6

RYOTEMOCHI IRIMI-NAGE

Uke utilizes a two hands on one wrist grab from *Gyaku-Hanmi* (photo #1).

APPLIED PRINCIPLES: Gliding powerfully to *Uke's* side, *Nage* lowers hips and aligns shoulder while pivoting to match *Uke's* original direction (photo #2). Throwing left leg back, *Nage* draws *Uke* sharply around while cutting right hand below *Uke's* arms (photo #3).

Stepping forward with left foot, *Nage* firmly grasps the nape of *Uke's* neck while extending right arm fully (photo #4). Lowering hips, *Nage* locks *Uke's* head tightly to right shoulder (photo #5). Throwing right leg back 180 degrees, *Nage* draws *Uke* around driving *Uke's* hips past center (photo #6, opposite page).

CONTINUED

6

First extending right arm powerfully forward, *Nage* then steps deeply behind *Uke* with right leg, taking solid control of the mutual center to implement *Irimi-Nage* throw (photos #7 #8).

7

OBSERVATION: Although *Irimi-Nage* at first appears to be a clash of power against power, strength against strength, such as an ax slamming its blade into the trunk of a tree, in actual application *Irimi-Nage* should be performed as a powerful torrent of water engulfing a tree in its path. Never standing to face the tree's power, it rushes effortlessly around the trunk, never lingering, never hampered, without malice it rips the tree free of its roots.

8

MAE-GERI IRIMI-NAGE *OYO WAZA*

1

2

3

PRE-NOTE: On this and the next two pages, we have chosen to concentrate on *Irimi-Nage Oyo Waza* as applied to a front and side kicking attack. It should be noted at the beginning of this sub-section, that there are numerous *Waza* which may be utilized to neutralize a kicking attack within the body of *Aikido*. Yet it should also be noted that *O'Sensei* did not formally develop or categorize specific *Waza* to this task. Therefore, it should be understood that kick defenses are not a part of the personal spiritual development process of *Aikido* as developed by *O'Sensei*, but merely a means by which a *Deshi* may become familiar with a form of aggression which he may face in today's society and at the same time stay healthy to follow his pursuit of the *Aiki*-spirit.

Aikido is an art which takes control of the attacker by exploiting his *Suki* (opening/weaknesses), be it direct or causing then absorbing the attacker from inside out. When an attacker lashes out with a kick, he is offering us a *Suki* which is easily defined, i.e. if it was meant for us to stand on one leg, that is all we would have been given; we should immediately take him to task and then bow deeply in gratitude.

Ueshiba of *Aikido* has no enemies, for when one comes to attack, he has already been defeated.   *O'SENSEI*

Uke utilizes front kick from *Ai-Hanmi* (photo #1).

APPLIED PRINCIPLES: Stepping forward and to the side with right foot, *Nage* cuts upward with *Tegatana* side of forearm, capturing *Uke's* leg (photo #2).

4

5

Rotating hips fully, *Nage* extends heel of right hand to *Uke's* chin (arm charged with *Kokyu*), driving *Uke's* balance behind center (photo #3, previous page). Maintaining full extension through arm, *Nage* steps in and behind *Uke's* left leg to execute throw, driving *Uke* completely to mat (photos #4, previous page & #5). Grasping *Uke's* right ankle with right hand, *Nage* pins lower leg firmly to chest while rotating hips powerfully clockwise, turning *Uke* over (photo #6). Stepping over *Uke* with left leg, *Nage* controls lower leg with left hand while locking knee to abdomen with right forearm. Engaging hips, *Nage* applies focused circular downward pressure into *Uke's* lower lumbar region (photo #7).

6

NOTE: *Nage* keeps right foot to the outside of *Uke's* left thigh, eliminating lateral movement.

OBSERVATION: *Aikido Waza* maintains powerful focus throughout a given throw or pin. *Ukemi* (art of receiving techniques) taken from a kicking attack is both extremely difficult and dangerous. So much so that we have found during public demonstrations, accompanied by the natural flow of adrenalin (in both *Uke* and *Nage*), that the incidence of injury has been too great to justify the continued inclusion of kick defenses. We now only teach this form of *Waza* to *Ikkyu* (first level) and *Yudansha* and forbid demonstration outside of the *Dojo*.

7

YOKO-GERI IRIMI-NAGE *OYO WAZA*

1

Uke utilizes side kick from *Gyaku-Hanmi* (photo #1).

APPLIED PRINCIPLES: As *Uke* steps in to deliver kick, *Nage* glides powerfully forward and to the inside of attack while deflecting *Uke's* right arm downward (photo #2). Leaning body inward, *Nage* draws *Uke's* balance to right (photo #3).

2

3

4

5

Extending right hand to base of *Uke's* jaw, *Nage* steps deeply behind *Uke* with right foot while grasping right arm firmly and drives powerfully to *Uke's* right rear corner (photos #4 #5). Allowing no leeway, *Nage* maintains full extension throughout throw, focusing on point just inside of forward foot (photo #6).

6

SHOMENUCHI IRIMI-NAGE OYO-NAGARE WAZA

1

2

PRE-NOTE: This *Oyo Waza* has been chosen to demonstrate the physical similarities in a side by side manner with the *Yoko Geri Irimi-Nage* on the previous page, but it should be noted that the true connection ultimately must be found within the properties manifest within the spirit of *Aiki* applied *Waza* and not the mere external appearance.

3

Uke utilizes either *Shomenuchi* (shown) or *Tsuki* attack (photo #1).

APPLIED PRINCIPLES: This *Ki No Nagare* (*Ki* flow) form of *Irimi-Nage* should be applied at *Toma* (*Uke* at two step distance). As *Uke* charges forward to close interval, *Nage* drives in opening hips fully. Taking upper sleeve, *Nage* draws *Uke* to a sharp 90 degree angle, off attacking line. Blasting forward and behind *Uke*, as if pulled forcefully from center (photo #2), *Nage* performs *Irimi-Nage* (photos #3 #4).

NOTE: This is a very rigorous form of *Nage Waza*. It is of utmost importance that *Uke's Ukemi* (art of receiving technique) be at a highly polished level.

4

KOKYU-NAGE

(BREATH THROW)

Literally translated as "breath throw," *Kokyu-Nage* is used essentially as a blanket term to cover a wide spectrum of *Waza* not having designated formal names. The many *Waza* carrying the name *Kokyu-Nage*, though seeming to have no singular physical characteristic in common, are nonetheless solidly connected by the omnipotent principles inherent in the application of *Kokyu-Ryoku* (breath power). Referring most often to *Waza* ending in the projection of *Uke*, *Kokyu-Nage* allows no room for head-on confrontation yet demands full connection of the spirit for proper application. It has been said that *O'Sensei* in his later years was capable of evading and throwing young, powerful *Uke* at will, seemingly with little or no physical contact. To begin to comprehend this, we must seek to cultivate the essence of *Kokyu-Ryoku* and strive to employ the principles of *Ki-No Musubi* (tying of *Ki*). Application of these principles should not be limited to only the raw energy of aggression but also utilized fully throughout all aspects of life. The countless manifestations of *Kokyu-Nage* provide us, through honest endeavor, with an important vehicle toward this development.

SHOMENUCHI KOKYU-NAGE *OYO-SUIGETSU WAZA*

APPLIED PRINCIPLES: Taking the initiative, *Nage* drives right *Tegatana* (handblade) toward *Uke's* face, forcing *Uke* to raise right hand to block (photos #1 #2). Shifting left foot to 90 degree angle, *Nage* unbalances *Uke* by cutting left forearm over right, taking control of *Uke's* wrist while fully extending arm and rotating hips forward (photos #3 #4).

Extending left arm beneath *Uke's* arm while stepping forward deeply with left foot, *Nage* locks *Uke's* elbow, driving *Uke* onto toes (photo #5). Rotating left *Tegatana* powerfully outward, *Nage* cuts *Uke* forward in large arcing motion, implementing throw (photo #6).

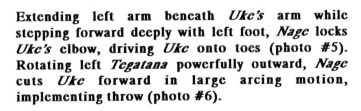

SHOMENUCHI KOKYU-NAGE *OYO-UCHI WAZA*

Uke utilizes overhead strike from *Gyaku-Hanmi* (photo #1).

APPLIED PRINCIPLES: Gliding forward, *Nage* meets *Uke's* attack (photo #2) as in *Shomenuchi Ikkyo Irimi* (see *Ikkyo* section). Stepping deeply forward with left foot, *Nage* removes outward extension from left arm and drives *Atemi* (left elbow) to *Uke's* jaw (photo #3).

Powerfully rotating and lowering hips clockwise, *Nage* extends arms fully while cutting in a large arcing motion to point just inside of forward foot, executing throw (photos #4 #5 #6).

NOTE: Demonstrated as *Kihon* (basic), this *Uchi Oyo Waza* may also be performed as *Ki-No Nagare* (Ki-flow), by moving rapidly from photo #1 to photo #4 with minimal contact and the elimination of *Atemi*.

SHOMENUCHI KOKYU-NAGE

1

2

Uke utilizes overhead strike from *Gyaku-Hanmi* (photo #1).

APPLIED PRINCIPLES: Gliding powerfully forward and to the outside of attack, *Nage* drives right arm upward, deflecting blow and taking control of centerline (photo #2). Stepping behind with left foot while taking *Uke's* neck with left hand, *Nage* pivots to join *Uke's* initial direction (photo #3).

3

4

Sharply throwing right foot back 180 degrees to rear, *Nage* draws *Uke* around, keeping head near shoulder and left elbow (*Nage's*) aligned with center (photos #4 #5). *Nage* cuts fully to *Uke's* rear with powerful, deeply based hip rotation as *Uke* passes *Nage's* axis (photos #6 #7).

5

6

7

OBSERVATION: Accompanying a strong attack is an exhalation, whereas inhalation accompanies attempted regaining of balance. *Nage* should take *Uke's* *Suki* (opening) and fill this void with applied *Waza*, literally, as *Uke* draws his breath.

SHOMENUCHI KOKYU-NAGE *OYO-KUBI WAZA*

Uke utilizes overhead strike from *Gyaku-Hanmi* (photo #1).

APPLIED PRINCIPLES: Gliding powerfully forward and to the outside of *Uke's* attack, *Nage* drives right arm up from center, deflecting the blow while taking control of the centerline (photo #2). See *Tai-Sabaki* section.

Grasping *Uke's* collar at nape of neck (or optionally pressing palm into kidney area of *Uke's* lower back), *Nage* steps across *Uke's* rear with left foot while placing right forearm up and under chin, locking neck between forearms (photo #3).

NOTE: *Nage's* forearm, wrist, and hand must be fully energized, with top of forearm facing underside of chin (thumb toward *Uke*, little finger away).

Stepping back with right foot, *Nage* throws *Uke* with deep engagement of hips to rear, while cutting behind and down *Uke's* back (photos #4 #5).

211

SHOMENUCHI KOKYU-NAGE *OYO-KUBI WAZA*

Uke utilizes overhead strike from *Ai-Hanmi* (photo #1).

APPLIED PRINCIPLES: *Nage* steps forward and to the inside of attack, taking a position at an angle 45 degrees to *Uke's* center (photo #2).

Driving forward and up from *Uke's* center to chin with left hand, *Nage* steps in with left foot and secures a hold on *Uke's* sleeve at elbow (photo #3). Cutting *Uke's* head back and to rear, *Nage* executes throw, completing cut to point just inside of forward foot (photos #4 #5).

NOTE: *Nage* must keep *Uke's* elbow in line with center and over *Nage's* forward foot. Execution of throw (photos #3 #4) should be accomplished in a one count, not a one-two count.

RYOKATATORI KOKYU-NAGE

1

Uke utilizes two lapel/shoulder grab from *Ai-Hanmi* (photo #1).

APPLIED PRINCIPLES: As *Uke* steps forward to grab, *Nage* extends left arm upward between *Uke's* arms while shifting right foot 45 degrees to the outside of line of attack (photo #2).

2

3

4

Slightly lowering and rotating hips counterclockwise, *Nage* cuts downward on inside of *Uke's* right elbow with left forearm while driving *Uke's* left inner elbow upward with right hand, breaking *Uke's* balance to right rear corner (photo #3). Keeping both arms fully extended, *Nage* drives right foot and hips deeply forward simultaneously cutting to point just inside of right foot, implementing throw (photos #4 #5).

NOTE: This *Kihon* (basic) may also be performed as *Ki-No Nagare* (*Ki*-flow) by elongating *Uke's* approach with a direct step back (from photo #2) followed by a 180 degree pivot, executing throw along initial line of attack.

5

YOKOMENUCHI KOKYU-NAGE

Uke utilizes side strike to head from *Ai-Hanmi* (photo #1).

1

2

3

4

5

6

APPLIED PRINCIPLES: Gliding in deeply as *Uke* steps forward with strike, *Nage* stops *Uke's* arm at point just below elbow while driving *Atemi* (heel of palm) to chin, breaking *Uke's* balance to left rear corner (photo #2, previous page). Capturing *Uke's* wrist with right hand, *Nage* draws left hand to point just below shoulder while stepping deeply behind *Uke* with left foot (photo #3, previous page). Cutting fully to point just inside of left foot, *Nage* executes throw while sliding left hand to inside of *Uke's* elbow (photos #4 #5, previous page).

7

Engaging hips, *Nage* drives elbow counterclockwise, turning *Uke* face down (photo #6). Moving right foot forward, *Nage* slips *Uke's* wrist into crook of right elbow while maintaining locking pressure to *Uke's* elbow (photo #7). Sitting down to straddle *Uke's* shoulder, *Nage* clamps arm tightly to chest while applying rotation toward *Uke's* head, concentrating on pinning the triangular area of *Uke's* breastbone just below the throat firmly to the mat (photo #8).

8

RYOTETORI KOKYU-NAGE

1

2

3

Uke utilizes two wrist grab from *Ai-Hanmi* (photo #1).

APPLIED PRINCIPLES: At point of contact, *Nage* steps forward and to the side with left foot, then throwing right foot back 270 degrees, draws *Uke* around (photos #2 #3).

4

5

6

Grasping *Uke's* wrists, *Nage* steps forward with right foot (photo #4). Pivoting and lowering hips powerfully counterclockwise while keeping elbows tight to body, *Nage* cuts to point just inside of left foot, implementing throw (photos #5 #6).

RYOKATATORI KOKYU-NAGE

1

2

3

Uke utilizes two lapel grab from *Ai-Hanmi* (photo #1).

APPLIED PRINCIPLES: Taking a half step forward with left foot, followed by a half step back with right foot, *Nage* delivers *Atemi* upward between *Uke's* arms to chin with left fist (photo #2). Extending left forearm up and outward against *Uke's* right inner elbow, *Nage* powerfully rotates hips toward *Uke* while driving downward on inside of *Uke's* left elbow with right forearm (photo #3).

4

5

Inserting right arm and upper body between arms while stepping forward to *Uke's* outside with right foot, *Nage* extends right arm upward beneath armpit while contacting *Uke's* right inner hip with left *Tegatana* (photo #4). Driving up and outward against *Uke's* hip, fully breaking *Uke's* balance to left rear corner, *Nage* rotates hip sharply clockwise cutting outward with right hand, implementing throw (photos #5 #6).

NOTE: Palms must face upward with shoulders remaining down, allowing throw to be executed from center.

6

USHIRO HIJITORI KOKYU-NAGE

1

Uke utilizes two rear elbow grab (photo #1).

APPLIED PRINCIPLES: Charging arms with strong *Kokyu*, *Nage* glides back to left rear corner while lowering hips (photo #2).

2

3

Engaging lower back/upper hip area fully across *Uke's* left arm (drawing *Uke's* balance onto left foot), *Nage* forms a large circle with arms (elbows facing outward) while beginning to rotate hips toward *Uke*, driving *Uke's* right elbow upward (photo #3). As right hip passes *Uke's* left hip, *Nage* steps deeply behind *Uke* with right foot, fully engaging *Uke's* body (photo #4). Continuing clockwise rotation, *Nage* executes throw to *Uke's* left rear corner (photos #5 #6).

4

NOTE: *Nage* must maintain hip positioning below that of *Uke's* center while keeping shoulders firmly down and not allowing head to follow *Uke's* fall (see *Kokyu-Ho, Kokyu Ryoku Taiso* section).

5

6

USHIRO RYOTETORI KOKYU-NAGE

Uke utilizes two rear wrist grab (photo #1).

APPLIED PRINCIPLES: Charging both arms with strong *Kokyu*, *Nage* screws/spirals both arms up and outward (keeping alignment with hips) while gliding back and under *Uke's* left arm to left rear corner, causing *Uke* to be drawn forward (photo #2). Engaging solid driving hip motion while maintaining powerful extension in both arms, *Nage* projects *Uke* forward, implementing throw (photo #3).

NOTE: *Nage* must maintain torso in an erect position, not bending forward or rounding back. Posture must be lowered only through bending of knees. Care should also be taken that *Nage* does not step back with inside foot (foot closest to *Uke*, photo #2) or balance will be severely compromised by *Uke's* forward momentum during throw.

OBSERVATION: This form of *Kokyu-Nage* may appear at first glance to be relatively easy to perform due to its simplicity of movement. In reality it is the embodiment of all the difficulties involved in the practice of *Kokyu-Nage* and *Aikido Waza* in general. Your mind, body, and spirit must be compressed into your *Seika-Tanden* (*Hara* or one-point, lower abdomen) and then powerfully sent forth through every pore in your body, firmly rooting you to the earth while allowing you to move freely, expanding as though to the heavens. The practice of this *Kokyu-Nage* in its *Kihon* (basic) form as shown can be both rewarding and frustrating. Until a strong understanding of its foundation has been acquired, the practice of this *Kokyu-Nage* as *Ki-No Nagare* (*Ki*-flow) should be shelved.

USHIRO RYOTETORI KOKYU-NAGE *NAGARE WAZA*

Uke utilizes a two rear wrist grab, starting from the side, then moving behind *Nage* to secure grip (photos #1 #2).

7

APPLIED PRINCIPLES: As *Uke* moves behind to secure second grip, *Nage* steps forward mirroring *Uke's* movement and breaking *Uke's* timing (photos #3 #4 opposite page). Allowing *Uke* to secure second grip, *Nage* pivots sharply and glides back and under *Uke's* right arm (photo #5 opposite page). Continuing to rotate hips counterclockwise, *Nage* draws *Uke* forward, crossing right arm over left (photo #6 opposite page).

8

Stepping with right foot deeply behind *Uke*, *Nage* lowers hips and raises right arm with elbow coming up from *Uke's* center to chin (photo #7). Extending right arm, *Nage* rotates hips powerfully clockwise and executes throw to rear (photos #8 #9). See *Kokyu-Ho*.

NOTE: This *Kokyu-Nage* is shown in a *Ki-No Nagare* (*Ki*-flow) form.

9

HIJI WAZA

(ELBOW TECHNIQUE)

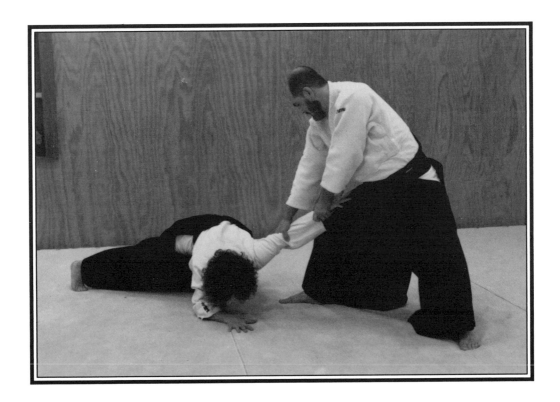

Literally translated as "elbow technique," the term *Hiji Waza* refers to techniques which are applied to the elbow in a direction opposed to its natural bend. Though the practice of *Hiji Waza* in *Aikido* seeks to control while not causing permanent injury to an aggressor, the capacity for just such an occurrence still remains. The prospect of dislocating or breaking the elbow joint with the application of as little as seven pounds of pressure demonstrates vividly the volatile properties inherent in *Hiji Waza*. Therefore, *Hiji Waza* demands that *Nage* exercise total and complete self-control, being ever vigilant to unfocused or disjointed movements of the mind as well as the body. Hence, the compelling nature of *Hiji Waza* necessitates sound and conscientious study.

OBSERVATION: The practice of *Hiji Waza* can clearly be seen in both the early *Kobukan* and *Iwama* periods of *O'Sensei's* development of *Aikido*. Yet *Hiji Waza* is excluded from the present curriculum of many *Aikido Dojo*. A reason for this exclusion may be the extreme difficulty found in safely teaching *Hiji Waza* to *Mudansha* (those below *Dan* rank). A more disturbing note is the watered-down pushing and pulling applications found in many non-traditional styles of *Aikido*. It is recommended this form of training be omitted until such time as proper personal instruction of *Hiji Waza* can be obtained.

KATATETORI HIJI-OSAE *IRIMI / OMOTE*

1

Uke utilizes straight hand grab from *Gyaku-Hanmi* (photo #1).

APPLIED PRINCIPLES: Gliding powerfully forward and to the outside of *Uke's* posture, *Nage* raises right arm while grasping *Uke's* wrist from below with left hand (photo #2).

2

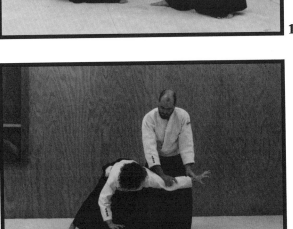

3

Freeing right hand from *Uke's* grip, *Nage* takes control of the back of *Uke's* elbow, then rotating hips counterclockwise, cuts *Uke's* arm downward (photo #3). Stepping forward forcefully with right foot, *Nage* drives *Uke* fully off balance (photo #4).

4

Drawing left leg up while pressing firmly downward on elbow, *Nage* drives *Uke* to mat. Continuing to solidly hold *Uke's* elbow to mat, *Nage* completes pin by lightly but firmly lifting *Uke's* wrist (photo #5).

NOTE: *Nage* must hold with palm squarely on the back of *Uke's* wrist just below joint (photo #2), rotating wrist so that *Uke's* thumb is facing forward at bottom of cutting motion (photo #3). It must be clearly understood that excessive and unnecessary pressure will dislocate or break *Uke's* elbow.

5

SHOMENUCHI HIJI-OSAE SUIGETSU WAZA

1

2

APPLIED PRINCIPLES: Taking the initiative, *Nage* glides forward in a left *Hanmi* while driving *Tegatana* (handblade) toward *Uke's* face, causing *Uke* to reflect *Nage's* movement (photos #1 #2).

3

At the point of contact, *Nage* encircles *Uke's* forearm (grasping the pulse side of wrist) while stepping back with left foot, drawing *Uke's* balance forward (photo #3).

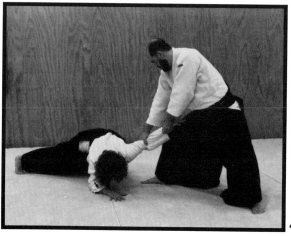

4

Grasping the back of *Uke's* elbow with right hand (thumb facing inward), *Nage* shifts hips back, drawing *Uke* onto forearm (photo #4). Keeping left hand in line with center, *Nage* presses firmly down on elbow, driving *Uke* to mat. *Nage* completes pin by continuing to lower hips (photo #5).

NOTE: *Nage* must rotate *Uke's* wrist so that palm is facing upward with thumb toward *Nage* (photo #3). Placement of *Uke's* shoulder must be just to the inside of *Nage's* right foot (photos #4 #5).

5

RYOTEMOCHI HIJI-NAGE

1

Uke utilizes a two hands on one wrist hold starting from a forearm touching block in *Ai-Hanmi* and moving to *Gyaku-Hanmi* twisting *Nage's* arm behind back (photos #1 #2).

APPLIED PRINCIPLES: Lowering and rotating hips counterclockwise with *Uke's* twisting motion, *Nage* steps back and in front of *Uke* with left foot. Powerfully extending left arm downward, *Nage* firmly grasps left wrist with right hand (photo #3).

2

3

4

5

Maintaining hips in a lowered position and strong downward extension in left arm, *Nage* continues powerful counterclockwise rotation, executing projection of *Uke* over left hip (photos #4 #5 #6).

NOTE: *Nage* must position body so as to hold *Uke's* left elbow locked against back, from right hip to point just below left shoulder (photos #3 #4).

6

HANTAI HIJI-NAGE

1

2

Uke utilizes a cross hand grab from *Ai-Hanmi* (photo #1).

APPLIED PRINCIPLES: Stepping forward to align right foot with *Uke's* left foot, *Nage* drives *Atemi* toward *Uke's* face (photo #2). Throwing left foot back 180 degrees to align hips with *Uke*, *Nage* brings right hand over and then beneath *Uke's* left arm (photo #3).

3

4

5

With the right hand grasping his own left wrist (just above *Uke's* hold), *Nage* extends hips upward while drawing left hand toward center (photo #4). Taking a small gliding step forward, *Nage* drives hips forward to execute throw simultaneously releasing *Uke* from joint lock (photos #5 #6).

NOTE: *Nage* must execute caution in placement of his forearm (photo #4). Placement above the back of the joint will cause elbow to dislocate or break.

6

TSUKI HIJI-NAGE

Uke utilizes a thrusting attack from *Ai-Hanmi* (photo #1).

APPLIED PRINCIPLES: As *Uke* strikes, *Nage* glides forward and to the outside of attack (photo #2).

Grasping *Uke's* wrist from above, *Nage* rotates *Uke's* arm clockwise until palm is facing upward. Pivoting hips powerfully clockwise, *Nage* drives upward against the back of *Uke's* elbow with left hand, causing *Uke* to raise onto toes (photo #3).

Driving hips forward while drawing right hand slightly downward and into line with center, *Nage* executes *Soto* (outside) throw by fully extending left arm along centerline created by hip rotation (photos #4 #5).

NOTE: *Nage* may execute *Atemi* to both the ribcage and the head at point of entry (photo #2).

229

YOKOMENUCHI HIJI-NAGE *UCHI*

1

Uke utilizes a side strike to the head from *Ai-Hanmi* (photo #1).

APPLIED PRINCIPLES: *Nage* executes inside entry (photos #2 #3). See *Yokomenuchi Shiho-Nage* for description.

2

3

4

5

6

7

Rotating *Uke's* palm upward, *Nage* steps forward with right foot, then throws left foot back 180 degrees while driving upward on *Uke's* elbow with right hand (photos #4 #5). Gliding forward and beneath *Uke's* arm, *Nage* pivots hips counterclockwise while cutting to point just inside of forward foot to execute throw (photos #6 #7).

YOKOMENUCHI HIJI-NAGE SOTO

1

Uke utilizes a side strike to the head from *Ai-Hanmi* (photo #1).

APPLIED PRINCIPLES: As *Uke* steps forward with attack, *Nage* glides to the outside while directing *Uke's* strike past and to the inside (photo #2).

NOTE: This entry is shown in *Ki-No Nagare* form. See *Yokomenuchi Kotegaeshi* for *Kihon* (basic) entry.

2

3

4

5

Cutting *Uke's* arm downward and into the center, *Nage* grasps the pulse side of *Uke's* wrist (photo #3). Gripping the back of *Uke's* elbow with the right hand (thumb facing upward), *Nage* steps deeply to the front of *Uke* with right foot executing throw (photos #4 #5 #6).

6

GANSEKI-OTOSHI
(HEELS OVER HEAD DROP)

MEN-NAGE
(HEAD THROW)

The first portion of this section deals with *Ganseki-Otoshi*. Translated for use in *Aikido* as "heels over head drop" or "boulder drop," *Ganseki-Otoshi* requires *Nage* to engage and throw in a virtual back to back position. Though *Aikido Waza* gains maximum effect from each ounce of applied effort, it should be noted that *Ganseki-Otoshi* demands upper body muscle tone, proper alignment of the spine, correct usage of the quadriceps, and its fair share of physical effort. An extremely rigorous throw, the safe execution of *Ganseki-Otoshi* requires thoroughly developed *Ukemi* (art of receiving, i.e. *Uke* - one who receives). Covered within the final portion of this section, the term *Men-Nage* translated means "head throw," and requires the projection of the attacker's body through the manipulation of his head. As with *Ganseki-Otoshi*, *Men-Nage* demands a fully developed level of *Ukemi*. Though seldom seen in present day *Dojo*, *Ganseki-Otoshi* and *Men-Nage* are nonetheless a vital component of traditional *Aikido* and must not be overlooked during advanced levels of training.

NOTE: As with *Hiji Waza* (elbow technique), *Men-Nage* evolved from *Waza* employed by the *Bushi* (warrior caste) for the purpose of rendering helpless and ultimately killing an opponent. Therefore it goes without saying that *Men-Nage* should be practiced only under the close personal supervision of a highly qualified instructor.

SHOMENUCHI GANSEKI-OTOSHI

Uke utilizes overhead strike from *Gyaku-Hanmi* (photo #1).

APPLIED PRINCIPLES: Controlling *Chushin* (centerline), *Nage* glides forward and to the outside deflecting strike with left arm (photo #2). Grasping nape of neck with right hand, *Nage* steps behind *Uke* with right foot while lowering body (photo #3).

Positioning left foot between *Uke's* legs, *Nage* applies *Tegatana* to back of *Uke's* right knee simultaneously drawing *Uke* backwards (photo #4). Engaging and driving hips beneath *Uke's* center, *Nage* implements throw from left hip to right shoulder (photos #5 #6).

NOTE: This page demonstrates second contacting hand application. See next page for first contacting hand application of *Ganseki-Otoshi*.

SHOMENUCHI GANSEKI-OTOSHI

Uke utilizes overhead strike from *Gyaku-Hanmi* (photo #1).

APPLIED PRINCIPLES: Gliding to the outside while deflecting strike, *Nage* grasps the back of *Uke's* collar with right hand while simultaneously driving left *Tegatana* to back of *Uke's* knee (photo #2).

Stepping forward placing left foot between *Uke's* feet, *Nage* throws right foot back 90 degrees (aligning with *Uke's* spine) while lowering hips and drawing *Uke* backwards (photo #3). Engaging and driving hips beneath *Uke's* center in a low to high arc while drawing downward on *Uke's* collar in a high to low arc, *Nage* executes throw from left hip to right shoulder (photos #4 #5).

NOTE: *Nage* must support *Uke* (at collar) until rotation of body is complete. Driving head to mat prior to full rotation exposes *Uke* to the risk of serious injury.

USHIRO KUBISHIME GANSEKI-OTOSHI

1

Uke utilizes a wrist and one arm strangle hold from the rear (photo #1).

APPLIED PRINCIPLES: Locking *Uke's* elbow to chest, *Nage* raises right hand while rotating hips to left (photo #2).

2

3

4

Stepping forward with right foot, *Nage* powerfully rotates hips toward *Uke* applying left *Tegatana* to elbow, breaking grip (photo #3). Grasping *Uke's* collar with left hand while driving right hand down and to the outside of *Uke's* right wrist to release grip, *Nage* steps behind *Uke* with right foot simultaneously lowering body and applying *Tegatana* to knee (photo #4). Throwing left foot back 90 degrees, *Nage* engages hip and slides beneath *Uke* implementing throw (photos #5 #6 #7).

5

6

7

GYAKU RYOKATATORI MEN-NAGE

1

Uke utilizes an opposite two lapel grip from *Ai-Hanmi* (photo #1).

APPLIED PRINCIPLES: Advancing right foot slightly forward and to the outside, *Nage* steps back with left foot while driving right *Atemi* upward between *Uke's* arms (photo #2). Engaging hips, *Nage* cuts downward with right *Tegatana* on the inside of *Uke's* elbow and applies *Atemi* to *Uke's* temple with left hand (photo #3).

2

3

4

5

Grasping the left side of *Uke's* head in a circular manner with left hand, *Nage* extends upward against *Uke's* chin with right palm (photo #4). Continuing powerful hip rotation, *Nage* executes throw as though elongating *Uke* from head to tailbone (photos #5 #6).

NOTE: Even a moment of hesitation by *Uke* in complying with application of *Men-Nage* can lead to serious injury.

6

USHIRO RYOKATATORI MEN-NAGE

Uke utilizes two rear lapel grab (photo #1).

APPLIED PRINCIPLES: Lowering hips while stepping back with right foot, *Nage* glides back and between *Uke's* arms and executes *Atemi* to *Uke's* face with left hand and abdomen with right hand (photo #2).

Moving left hand over *Uke's* head in circular manner, *Nage* extends upward against chin with right hand (photo #3). With an outward extending motion emanating from hips, *Nage* implements throw (photos #4 #5).

NOTE: *Nage* may assist *Uke's* fall by lightly cupping head during mid-portion of body rotation.

OBSERVATION: Perform *Ukemi* as though rolling effortlessly up and over a cloud with no desire to break or disrupt its form.

KATATORI MEN-NAGE

1

Uke utilizes a one hand lapel grab from *Gyaku-Hanmi* (photo #1).

APPLIED PRINCIPLES: Shifting body forward and to the outside, *Nage* draws *Uke's* elbow into line with center while applying *Atemi* to face with left hand (photo #2).

2

3

4

5

6

Crossing in front of *Uke* with left foot, *Nage* drives left palm upward against chin while grasping right rear portion of *Uke's* head with right hand (photo #3). Throwing right foot back 90 degrees, *Nage* powerfully rotates hips clockwise executing projection as though elongating *Uke's* spine (photos #4 #5 #6).

YOKOMENUCHI MEN-NAGE

1

Uke utilizes strike to side of head from *Ai-Hanmi* (photo #1).

APPLIED PRINCIPLES: Gliding forward and to the outside, *Nage* meets *Uke's* attacking arm with right arm and immediately directs it down and into centerline with left *Tegatana* (photos #2 #3).

2

3

4

5

Driving across the front of *Uke* with left foot, *Nage* extends upward against chin with left hand while grasping right rear side of *Uke's* head with right hand (photo #4). Throwing right foot back 90 degrees, *Nage* projects outward while powerfully rotating hips clockwise to implement throw (photos #5 #6).

6

TANTO-TORI

(KNIFE TAKING)

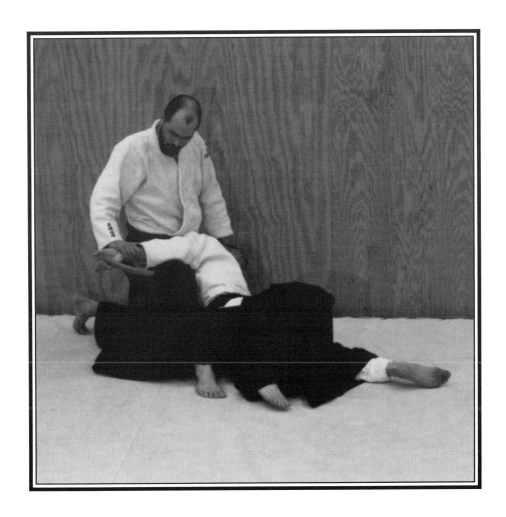

Translated within the context of *Aikido* as "knife taking," *Tanto-Tori* refers to technique employed against a knife-wielding attacker. As has been stated earlier, the roots of *Aikido* may be traced to the ancient arts developed by the Japanese *Bushi*, both in armed and unarmed combat as well as empty-handed confrontation with an armed attacker. It is a sad commentary that in today's society, training to protect oneself against assault with a deadly weapon is still necessary. Dealing with a *Tanto*-wielding *Uke* affords *Nage* the opportunity to learn to deal with this kind of situation in the controlled environment of the *Dojo*. Just as the term *Tanto-Tori* indicates, the practice of Traditional *Aikido* mandates the knife always be removed from the possession of the attacker. Control, speed, and clarity of thought and action are only by-products of the deeper understanding of *Aikido* which *Tanto-Tori* can provide with frequent diligent training.

TSUKI KOTEGAESHI

1

Uke utilizes a stabbing attack to the mid-section from *Ai-Hanmi* (photo #1).

APPLIED PRINCIPLES: Moving forward and to the outside, *Nage* deflects attacking arm (photo #2). Throwing right foot back, *Nage* draws *Uke* around and off balance (photo #3).

2

3

4

Throwing left leg back, *Nage* turns *Uke's* wrist back and over forearm, focusing control on *Tanto* (photos #4 #5). Moving right hand to inside of *Uke's* elbow, *Nage* applies circular pressure downward, turning *Uke* over (photo #6). With left leg bracing arm and right foot placed forward of *Uke's* left shoulder, *Nage* drives downward on back of hand while relieving *Uke* of *Tanto* with right hand (photo #7).

5

6

7

TSUKI GOKYO *TENKAN / URA*

Uke utilizes stabbing attack to the mid-section from *Ai-Hanmi* (photo #1).

APPLIED PRINCIPLES: As *Uke* steps forward with thrust, *Nage* simultaneously steps forward and to *Uke's* right with left foot, then draws right foot back and off line of attack while taking *Uke's* wrist from above with left hand (photo #2). Raising *Uke's* arm, *Nage* steps forward aligning right foot with *Uke's* left (photo #3). Throwing left foot back, *Nage* rotates hips counterclockwise, cutting *Uke* sharply to left rear corner (photo #4).

Pinning *Uke* to mat, *Nage* applies *Yonkyo* at point of separation of wrist and forearm while drawing wrist in and underneath elbow. Applying pressure to back of elbow, *Nage* removes *Tanto* from *Uke's* grasp (photos #5 #6).

SHOMENUCHI GOKYO *IRIMI / OMOTE*

Uke utilizes overhead stabbing attack from *Gyaku-Hanmi* (photo #1).

APPLIED PRINCIPLES: Stepping forward with right foot, *Nage* moves off line of attack while stopping *Uke's* elbow with right hand and taking *Gokyo* grip with left hand (photo #2). Rotating hips counterclockwise while driving forward with left foot, *Nage* cuts arm down and into center, breaking *Uke's* balance forward (photo #3).

Stepping deeply forward with right foot, *Nage* drives *Uke's* weight onto right arm (photo #4). Drawing left leg up, *Nage* pins *Uke* firmly to mat (photo #5). Applying strong *Yonkyo* pressure to point at separation of wrist and forearm, *Nage* draws wrist up and underneath elbow. Directing pressure downward on *Uke's* elbow (aimed at inner knuckles of open palm), *Nage* simultaneously removes *Tanto* from *Uke's* grasp (photo #6).

SHOMENUCHI GOKYO *TENKAN / URA*

1

Uke utilizes overhead stabbing attack from *Gyaku-Hanmi* (photo #1).

APPLIED PRINCIPLES: Stepping forward to align left foot with *Uke's* advancing right foot, *Nage* shifts body off line of attack while stopping downward movement of *Uke's* arm with left hand at point just above elbow (photo #2). Grasping *Uke's* wrist (palm to pulse with thumb facing upward) with right hand, *Nage* throws right foot back and cuts sharply to right rear corner (photo #3).

2

3

Lowering center, *Nage* pins *Uke* firmly to mat (photo #4). Driving *Yonkyo* pressure deeply into point at separation of wrist and forearm while drawing wrist in and underneath elbow, *Nage* applies strong pressure to back of *Uke's* elbow (directed at inner knuckles of open palm) while removing *Tanto* from *Uke's* grasp (photo #5).

4

5

YOKOMENUCHI GOKYO *TENKAN/URA*

1

Uke utilizes stabbing attack to side of neck/upper body from *Ai-Hanmi* (photo #1).

APPLIED PRINCIPLES: Gliding powerfully forward (extending arms with *Kokyu*), *Nage* stops *Uke's* attacking arm at point just below elbow while applying *Atemi* to face with right hand (photo #2).

2

3

4

5

Grasping *Uke's* wrist (palm to pulse), *Nage* directs arm down and into center with a sharp clockwise rotation of hips (photos #3 #4). Pinning *Uke* to mat, *Nage* applies *Yonkyo* at point of separation of wrist and forearm. Drawing wrist in and underneath elbow, *Nage* applies pressure to back of elbow (directed toward inner knuckles of open palm) while relieving *Uke* of *Tanto* (photos #5 #6).

6

KATATORI SHOMENUCHI GOKYO *IRIMI/OMOTE*

1

Uke utilizes lapel grab and overhead stabbing attack from *Gyaku-Hanmi* (photo #1).

APPLIED PRINCIPLES: Offsetting right foot to a 90 degree angle, *Nage* moves out of line of attack while taking elbow with right hand and *Gokyo* grip of *Uke's* wrist with left hand (photo #2).

2

3

5

4

Cutting *Uke* sharply, *Nage* steps deeply forward, draws left foot up and pins *Uke* firmly to mat, removing *Tanto* from *Uke's* grasp (photos #3 #4 #5 #6). See *Shomenuchi Gokyo Irimi*.

6

SHOMENUCHI KUBI-WAZA

1

Uke utilizes overhead stabbing attack from *Gyaku-Hanmi* (photo #1).

APPLIED PRINCIPLES: As *Uke* steps in striking downward, *Nage* steps forward and to the outside of attack with left foot, deflecting attacking forearm with right arm (photo #2).

2

3

Encircling *Uke's* neck with left arm, *Nage* throws right leg back 180 degrees, taking a position directly behind *Uke's* center while drawing *Uke's* arm down with firm grip on pulse region (photo #3).

4

Stepping straight back with left leg, *Nage* lowers *Uke* to mat. Positioning elbow over leg, *Nage* releases neck hold and applies pressure to carotid artery on right side of *Uke's* neck while applying downward pressure at wrist, causing *Uke* to drop *Tanto* (photo #4). Taking control of wrist with left hand, *Nage* shifts arm to the left while retrieving *Tanto* (photo #5).

NOTE: *Kubi Waza* is applied with back of hand drawing *Uke's* jaw to side and away from center as forearm drives in and downward at base of throat. Hips must be driven slightly forward at point of strongest application (see photo #3).

5

YOKOMENUCHI SHIHO-NAGE *IRIMI/OMOTE*

Uke utilizes slashing attack to side of neck/shoulder area from *Ai-Hanmi* (photo #1).

APPLIED PRINCIPLES: As *Uke* steps forward with attack, *Nage* steps in deeply with right foot. Deflecting arm holding *Tanto* with left forearm, *Nage* drives *Atemi* powerfully to *Uke's* face (photo #2). Throwing left leg back, *Nage* simultaneously cuts *Uke's* arm circularly down and into center while taking firm grip of *Uke's* wrist with both hands (photo #3).

Controlling the angle of the *Tanto*, *Nage* directs *Uke's* arm past center and glides forward with right foot (photo #4). Stepping forward (beneath *Uke's* arm with left foot), *Nage* pivots sharply back toward *Uke's* shoulder. Placing thumb of left hand squarely in the palm of *Uke's* hand, *Nage* peels the *Tanto* free as *Uke's* grip weakens during application of throw (photos #5 #6).

YOKOMENUCHI HIJI-NAGE

1

Uke utilizes stabbing attack to side of head/shoulder area from *Ai-Hanmi* (photo #1).

APPLIED PRINCIPLES: Stepping deeply to the inside as *Nage* steps forward with attack, *Nage* blocks *Uke's* lower forearm with left arm while applying *Atemi* to mid-section (photo #2).

2

3

5

Directing *Uke's* attacking arm down and to the front, *Nage* takes secondary grip with right hand (photo #3). Stepping forward to align left foot with *Uke's* right, *Nage* positions *Uke's* elbow just forward of shoulder while drawing downward on wrist raising *Uke* onto toes (photo #4). Throwing right leg back, *Nage* lowers hips while repositioning arm to right shoulder (photo #5).

6

Drawing down severely on wrist, causing *Uke* to loosen grip, *Nage* relieves *Uke* of *Tanto* with left hand (photo #6). Lowering hips, *Nage* shifts *Uke's* arm to point just below shoulder at top of bicep area, keeping *Uke* on toes with pressure at elbow (photo #7).

7

8

Driving forward to break *Uke's* balance, *Nage* projects *Uke* toward mat (photos #8 #9).

NOTE: *Nage* may perform *Chudan Giri* (mid-level cut) as *Uke* passes blade by drawing *Tanto* sharply outward against ribcage at point of projection (photo #8).

9

TSUKI KAITEN-KIME

1

Uke utilizes stabbing attack to the mid-section from *Ai-Hanmi* (photo #1).

APPLIED PRINCIPLES: Retaining left *Hanmi* while moving laterally to outside of attack (no advancement), *Nage* strikes *Uke's* wrist with left *Tegatana* (photo #2). Directing *Uke's* arm past center while gripping wrist, *Nage* steps forward with right foot while suppressing *Uke's* head with right hand (photo #3).

2

3

4

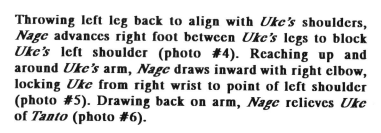

5

Throwing left leg back to align with *Uke's* shoulders, *Nage* advances right foot between *Uke's* legs to block *Uke's* left shoulder (photo #4). Reaching up and around *Uke's* arm, *Nage* draws inward with right elbow, locking *Uke* from right wrist to point of left shoulder (photo #5). Drawing back on arm, *Nage* relieves *Uke* of *Tanto* (photo #6).

6

TSUKI HIJI-KIME

1

Uke utilizes stabbing attack to the mid-section from *Ai-Hanmi* (photo #1).

APPLIED PRINCIPLES: Gliding forward and to the outside, *Nage* deflects attacking arm (photo #2). Grasping the back of *Uke's* wrist with right hand, *Nage* encircles elbow with right arm. Drawing *Uke's* arm across chest positioning *Tanto* harmlessly above shoulder, *Nage* throws left foot back 90 degrees driving *Uke* forward and off balance (photo #3).

2

3

Raising left arm upward from below *Uke's* wrist, *Nage* locks *Uke's* arm firmly to upper torso. Bringing left foot forward at a 45 degree angle to *Uke's* shoulders, *Nage* executes *Hiji-Kime* (photo #4).

OBSERVATION: In the employment of *Hiji Waza* (elbow techniques), the elbow becomes the entry point for *Kihaku* (projecting the spirit beyond the physical body). Therefore, it is important to keep in mind that *Hiji-Kime* (elbow-focus) is the application of self-control not the simple crippling of an attacker's limb.

4

HANMI-HANDACHI WAZA
(HALF-BODY HALF-STANDING TECHNIQUES)

Literally translated as "half-body half-standing," *Hanmi-Handachi* refers to a medium of practice in which *Nage* receives *Uke's* standing attack from a seated position. Virtually all techniques within the body of *Aikido* may be, and should be, practiced in *Hanmi-Handachi* form. Initially developed by the *Bushi* (warrior caste) to respond to sudden attack while in a seated position, the benefit of this form of training to the present day *Aiki-Deshi* (student of *Aikido*) is its ability, as with *Suwari Waza*, to stabilize the hips as well as strengthen movement from the *Seika-Tanden* (center). In addition, *Hanmi-Handachi* gives us a powerful medium through which to explore and learn how, when, and where to employ this strength and stability against one of much greater size than ourselves; working in, under, and around weight which is for the most part above our center of gravity.

OBSERVATION: Over the last ten years or so, there has developed a disturbing trend within many schools of *Aikido* and *Aiki* related arts, to drop both *Hanmi-Handachi* and *Suwari Waza* (see next section) from their training requirements. Regardless of the reason for the exclusion of these *Waza* - be it the lack of the instructor's comprehension of their significance, or because of the painful burden of exertion placed on the knees and legs - this kind of elimination of a vital part of training can only serve as an obstacle to understanding the art of *Aikido* as handed down by *O'Sensei*. Therefore, the responsibility is placed upon each and every *Aiki-Deshi*, instructor or student, to thoroughly explore the full spectrum of application of both *Hanmi-Handachi* and *Suwari Waza* in earnest.

KATATETORI KOKYU-NAGE *SOTO WAZA*

1

Uke utilizes straight hand grab from *Gyaku-Hanmi* (photo #1).

APPLIED PRINCIPLES: Gliding slightly forward and to the outside, *Nage* joins the forward movement of *Uke's* grasp, driving left *Tegatana* (handblade) up and to the outside (little finger side) of *Uke's* wrist (photo #2).

2

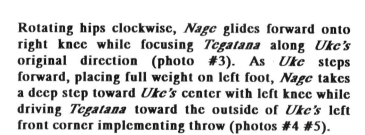

3

4

Rotating hips clockwise, *Nage* glides forward onto right knee while focusing *Tegatana* along *Uke's* original direction (photo #3). As *Uke* steps forward, placing full weight on left foot, *Nage* takes a deep step toward *Uke's* center with left knee while driving *Tegatana* toward the outside of *Uke's* left front corner implementing throw (photos #4 #5).

NOTE: These forms of *Kokyu-Nage* are of extreme value in that they not only show us but also help us to develop the proper flow of *Kokyu* energy, while at the same time allowing us to experience the necessity of *Ki-Musubi* (tying of *Ki* with that of the *Uke*) throughout the complete *Waza*.

5

KATATETORI KOKYU-NAGE *OYO-KOSHI WAZA*

1

Uke utilizes straight hand grab from *Gyaku-Hanmi* (photo #1).

APPLIED PRINCIPLES: Gliding forward to meet grab, *Nage* shifts *Uke's* arm slightly off center while stepping forward, placing left knee directly in front of *Uke* (photos #2 #3).

2

3

4

5

Guiding *Uke's* arm in an arcing motion, *Nage* shifts weight from left to right hip executing throw (photos #4 #5 #6).

NOTE: *Nage* does not physically engage *Uke's* body with hips to execute throw.

6

TSUKI KOTEGAESHI

1

Uke utilizes thrusting attack from *Ai-Hanmi* (photo #1).

APPLIED PRINCIPLES: Gliding forward and to the outside, *Nage* deflects and aligns with direction of *Uke's* attack (photo #2). Throwing right knee back, *Nage* draws *Uke's* balance around, causing *Uke* to step forward with left foot (photo #3).

2

3

4

5

6

Reinforcing *Kotegaeshi* grip with right hand, *Nage* takes a large glide step toward *Uke's* right rear corner with left knee (photo #4). Engaging hips fully, *Nage* cuts sharply to point just inside of left knee implementing throw (photos #5 #6).

NOTE: *Nage* must seek to control complete movement of *Uke's* arm, not merely twist wrist to effect throw.

SHOMENUCHI KOKYU-NAGE *UCHI WAZA*

Uke utilizes overhead strike from *Gyaku-Hanmi* (photo #1).

APPLIED PRINCIPLES: As *Uke* steps forward to strike, *Nage* glides deeply to the inside with right knee, raising right forearm to meet attack while driving left arm up and to the inside of *Uke's* elbow (photo #2).

1

2

3

4

At the point of contact with *Uke's* attack, *Nage* rotates hips counterclockwise, preparing to step in *Uke's* original direction with left knee while directing strike past with left arm (photo #3). Gliding forward onto left knee while cutting powerfully downward with left arm, *Nage* applies sharp *Atemi* toward *Uke's* face with right *Tegatana* executing throw (photo #4).

NOTE: *Nage* should pass suddenly to the inside of *Uke*, allowing and then reinforcing the continuation of the downward motion of the attack. There must be no point of initial resistance by *Nage*.

YOKOMENUCHI SHIHO-NAGE *IRIMI / OMOTE*

1

Uke utilizes strike to side of head from *Ai-Hanmi* (photo #1).

APPLIED PRINCIPLES: Stepping deeply forward with right knee, *Nage* deflects attacking arm with left forearm while driving *Atemi* to *Uke's* face with right *Tegatana* (photo #2).

2

3

Throwing left knee back, *Nage* directs *Uke's* arm in a circular pattern, breaking *Uke's* balance to right front corner (photo #3). Taking *Shiho-Nage* grip (left hand on top, right hand beneath), *Nage* glides right knee powerfully forward while rotating back of *Uke's* hand upward (photo #4).

4

5

Nage steps deeply forward with left knee (beneath attacking arm) while continuing to rotate *Uke's* wrist, causing counterclockwise rotation of *Uke's* body away from *Nage's* advance (photo #5). As left knee contacts ground, *Nage* pivots sharply back to *Uke's* shoulder while slightly raising right knee (photo #6). Making a small gliding motion forward with right knee, *Nage* executes throw by cutting firmly to point just inside of right knee (photos #7 #8).

6

7

OBSERVATION: As a giant flywheel that turns the pumps of an oil rig has a top and bottom to its stroke, but does not linger, continually allowing its weight to pump it from one movement into the next, so should *Nage* use the pumping motion of *Shikko* (knee-walking) movement without hesitation to move freely and powerfully throughout the application of all *Hanmi-Handachi Waza*.

8

RYOKATATORI HIJI-NAGE *OYO WAZA*

1

Uke utilizes two lapel grab from *Gyaku-Hanmi* (photo #1).

APPLIED PRINCIPLES: As *Uke* contacts lapels, *Nage* raises both hands (palms up, thumbs to the outside) engaging *Uke's* arms just below elbows (photo #2).

2

3

4

5

Driving upward locking *Uke's* elbows, *Nage* glides powerfully forward and beneath *Uke* executing throw (photos #3 #4 #5 #6).

6

RYOTETORI KOKYU-NAGE OYO WAZA

Uke utilizes two wrist hold from *Gyaku-Hanmi* (photo #1).

APPLIED PRINCIPLES: Blending with *Uke's* inertia at point of contact, *Nage* steps back deeply with right leg, drawing *Uke's* balance forward (photo #2). Rotating hips clockwise, *Nage* engages left *Soto-Tegatana* (outside handblade) to *Uke's* right wrist and right *Uchi-Tegatana* (inside handblade) to *Uke's* left wrist (photo #3).

1

2

3

4

Completing step with right knee, *Nage* cuts left hand toward *Uke's* face while cutting right hand to center executing throw (photos #4 #5).

NOTE: *Uke* may be permitted to roll free or *Nage* may retain arm (as shown photos #4 #5) and apply any of a number of *Katame Waza*. See *Katame Waza* section.

5

KATATETORI KOKYU-NAGE *OYO WAZA*

1

Uke utilizes straight hand grab from *Gyaku-Hanmi* (photo #1).

APPLIED PRINCIPLES: Gliding forward to pick up *Uke's* forward inertia (photo #2), *Nage* pivots hips to align with *Uke's* direction (photo #3). Turning palm upward to suppress *Uke's* grabbing hand, *Nage* begins to lead *Uke* around 180 degrees (photos #4 #5).

2

3

4

5

6

7

As *Uke* completes step with left foot, *Nage* glides forward and to *Uke's* right outside corner (photo #5). Stepping deeply forward with right leg. *Nage* engages inner elbow with right hand (photo #6). Driving elbow to *Uke's* right rear corner, *Nage* cuts powerfully to point just inside of forward knee (photos #7 #8).

8

USHIRO KUBISHIME KOKYU-NAGE

1

1

Uke utilizes one wrist grab and one arm strangle hold from rear, approaching *Nage* from side (photo #1).

APPLIED PRINCIPLES: Drawing held (left) wrist into center, *Nage* shifts hips toward *Uke's* attacking direction (photo #2).

2

Guiding *Uke's* left arm overhead, *Nage* extends right arm beneath *Uke's* right elbow while drawing left arm inward locking *Uke's* arms to chest (photo #3). Shifting hips forcefully to right front corner, *Nage* executes throw (photos #4 #5).

3

4

NOTE: Blending properly with the timing of *Uke's* step to the rear allows *Nage* the opportunity to execute the most powerful throw.

OBSERVATION: Mental image: enter as though inhaling *Uke*; execute as though exhaling *Uke*.

5

USHIRO RYOKATATORI KOKYU-NAGE OYO WAZA

1

2

3

Uke utilizes two rear lapel grab, approaching *Nage* from side (photo #1).

APPLIED PRINCIPLES: Meeting *Uke's* first contact with fully energized body, *Nage* makes firm connection with *Uke* (photo #2). Shifting right knee forward as *Uke* grabs lapel with second hand, *Nage* engages both arms powerfully forward (photo #3). Drawing left knee forward while rotating hips 45 degrees clockwise, *Nage* places both hands firmly to mat and bows vigorously forward implementing throw (photos #4 #5).

4

NOTE: *Nage* must seek to keep *Uke* taut throughout engagement, not allowing slack to appear within attack and subsequent response.

OBSERVATION: It is said that within *Aikido* one can develop the sixth sense (premonition - precognition etc.). Is it not possible that this so called sixth sense is none other than the full and proper usage of all our senses, awake and alive to the moment at hand? Utilizing all senses optimally, envelop and engage the *Uke* with mind, body, and spirit. *Uke* and moment are one and the same, moment and lifetime are one and the same -- *Katsuhayabi* (moment of swift victory).

5

SUWARI WAZA
(SEATED TECHNIQUES)

Literally translated as "seated technique," *Suwari Waza* refers to a medium of practice in which *Nage*, from a seated position, receives *Uke's* attack which is launched also from a seated position. *Suwari Waza* uses the knee walking exercise *Shikko* (see *Shikko* section) as a means of locomotion. Taken from the Japanese warrior's necessity to be prepared to defend or counter attack, even while in a seated position, *Suwari Waza* has evolved into an empty-handed form with the primary purpose of developing powerful hip and lower body strength as well as fluid centered motion.

NOTE: As stated in the observation on the first page of the *Hanmi-Handachi Waza* section, *Suwari Waza* is a form of practice which should not be overlooked but instead must be explored in earnest.

SHOMENUCHI IKKYO *IRIMI / OMOTE SUIGETSU WAZA*

1

APPLIED PRINCIPLES: Starting from a face to face seated position (photo #1), *Nage* takes the initiative driving left *Tegatana* (handblade) toward *Uke's* face while moving center forward (photo #2). Firmly taking hold of *Uke's* elbow with right hand, *Nage* grasps the pulse side of *Uke's* wrist while gliding powerfully forward with left leg (photo #3). Rotating hips counterclockwise while cutting fully downward, *Nage* draws right knee up pinning *Uke* to mat (photo #4).

2

3

NOTE: The application of *Suigetsu* both can and should be explored through *Ikkyo, Nikyo, Sankyo,* and *Yonkyo Waza* in both *Tachi* (standing) and *Suwari* (seated) forms. This section demonstrates *Ikkyo* as *Suigetsu Waza* and *Nikyo* and *Sankyo* with *Uke* initiating attack.

4

SHOMENUCHI IKKYO *TENKAN/URA SUIGETSU WAZA*

1

APPLIED PRINCIPLES: Starting from a face to face seated position (photo #1). Taking the initiative, *Nage* drives right *Tegatana* toward *Uke's* face simultaneously taking firm hold of *Uke's* blocking arm at point just above elbow with left hand (photo #2).

NOTE: It is important that *Nage* position *Uke's* elbow in line with *Uke's* center (spine). This allows *Nage* to take full control of *Uke's* balance and to freely direct *Uke's* movement. See photo #2 & *Ikkyo* section of *Tachi Waza* (standing technique).

2

3

Throwing right leg back, *Nage* cuts sharply to *Uke's* right rear corner (photo #3). Keeping *Uke's* elbow directly in line with center throughout turn, *Nage* pins *Uke* firmly to mat (photo #4). See *Katame Waza* section.

OBSERVATION: As with the practice of all *Waza*, one should think of the totality of the movement and attempt to remove the segmentation of thought and action, even at the level of beginner.

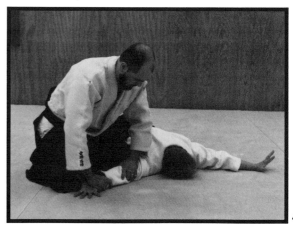

4

SHOMENUCHI NIKYO *TENKAN/URA*

1

Uke utilizes overhead strike from *Ai-Hanmi* (photo #1).

APPLIED PRINCIPLES: Stepping forward and to the outside, *Nage* deflects attack with left hand while taking hold of *Uke's* wrist from below with right hand (photo #2). Throwing left leg back 90 degrees, *Nage* breaks *Uke's* balance down and into center (photo #3).

2

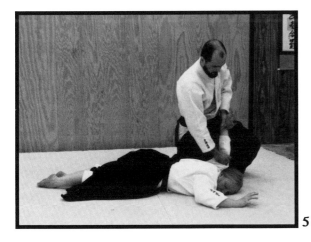

3

4

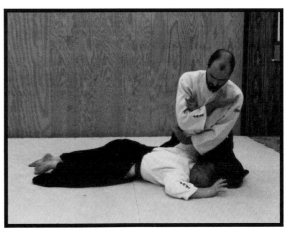

5

Rotating left thumb down and inside of *Uke's* thumb, *Nage* grips back of hand, drawing *Uke's* wrist up and into right shoulder for *Nikyo* application (photo #4). Shifting right hand to back of *Uke's* elbow, *Nage* drives shoulder to mat (photo #5). Stepping up with left leg to straddle arm, *Nage* positions *Uke's* wrist inside of right elbow and performs pin (photo #6). See *Katame Waza* section.

6

1

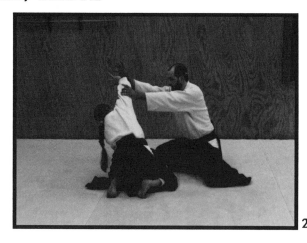

2

3

Uke utilizes overhead strike from *Gyaku-Hanmi* (photo #1).

APPLIED PRINCIPLES: Gliding powerfully forward and to the inside, *Nage* applies *Ikkyo Waza* (photo #2). See *Shomenuchi Ikkyo, Tachi Waza* (standing technique) section. Rotating hips clockwise, *Nage* cuts *Uke's* shoulder to within inches of mat (photo #3).

4

Driving forward with left leg, *Nage* places *Uke's* weight on *Uke's* left arm (photo #4). Sliding hand down and to the inside of *Uke's* arm, *Nage* takes firm *Sankyo* grip with left hand (photo #5). See *Sankyo, Tachi Waza* section.

5

6

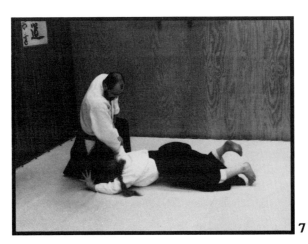

7

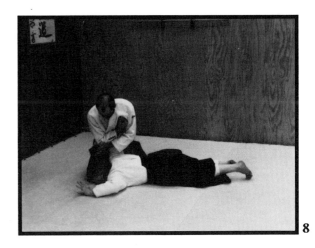

8

Taking a large circular step forward with right leg, *Nage* rotates *Uke's* wrist counterclockwise while applying *Atemi* to face with right hand (photo #6). Continuing to rotate wrist while cutting sharply across center, *Nage* straightens *Uke's* arm applying pressure to inside of elbow with right hand, pinning *Uke's* shoulder to mat (photo #7). Reaching up with right hand, *Nage* changes gripping hand and lowers left knee into *Uke's* side at armpit executing *Sankyo* pin (photo #8). See *Katame Waza* section.

HANTAI YONKYO *IRIMI/OMOTE*

Uke utilizes a cross hand grab from *Ai-Hanmi* (photo #1).

APPLIED PRINCIPLES: Raising left *Tegatana* (handblade) upward and to the outside of *Uke's* grasp, *Nage* glides forward with left knee while taking control of elbow with right hand and cuts *Uke's* arm down and into center (photos #2 #3).

Driving forward with right knee, *Nage* places bend in *Uke's* arm (photo #4). Bringing right hand down and to the inside of *Uke's* wrist, *Nage* advances right knee once again while directing *Uke's* elbow toward mat with sharp hip rotation (photos #5 #6). Stepping forward onto left foot, *Nage* continues to apply *Yonkyo* pressure while directing elbow toward left heel (photo #7).

KATATORI KOKYU-NAGE OYO WAZA

1

Uke utilizes one lapel/shoulder grab from *Ai-Hanmi* (photos #1 #2).

APPLIED PRINCIPLES: As *Uke* steps forward with right knee, *Nage* matches movement by taking a deep step back with left knee while deflecting grabbing hand with left *Tegatana* (photo #3). With both knees firmly planted, *Nage* lowers hips while cutting powerfully downward on *Uke's* elbow with right hand (photo #4).

2

3

4

5

Gripping *Uke's* wrist with right hand while placing right elbow inside *Uke's* elbow and wrist in bend of left elbow, *Nage* steps forward with left knee executing turnover (photo #5). *Nage* then applies *Katame Waza* (formal ending) with a smooth positive clockwise rotation in the direction of *Uke's* left ear (photo #6).

NOTE: This *Waza* and the two which follow demonstrate, in order, the principles of drawing, entering to the outside (rear), and entering to the inside (front) of *Uke's* line of attack.

6

YOKOMENUCHI KOKYU-NAGE *SOTO WAZA*

Uke utilizes strike to side of head from *Ai-Hanmi* (photo #1).

APPLIED PRINCIPLES: Gliding forward with left leg, *Nage* drives arms up and outward with powerful *Kokyu* and engages *Uke's* attack at point before accumulated release of attacking energy (photo #2). Rotating hips counterclockwise while maintaining low shoulder and hip association, *Nage* cuts simultaneously with both arms performing throw (photo #3).

NOTE: *Nage* engages *Uke's* arm at point just below joint of elbow. In this position *Nage* will be able to stop a very powerful attack while at the same time controlling *Uke's* center. *Nage* must be careful to rotate inside portion of forearm toward *Uke* at point of contact, at the same time maintaining elbows at a downward angle.

YOKOMENUCHI KOKYU-NAGE *UCHI WAZA*

1

Uke utilizes strike to the side of head from *Ai-Hanmi* (photo #1).

APPLIED PRINCIPLES: As *Uke* steps forward to deliver strike, *Nage* steps deeply to the inside of *Uke* with right leg, deflecting attacking hand outward and around *Nage* with left *Tegatana* (handblade) while delivering strong *Atemi* to *Uke's* face with right *Tegatana* (photo #2). Maintaining full engagement with *Uke*, *Nage* throws left leg back 180 degrees while cutting *Uke* powerfully to mat (photo #3).

2

3

OBSERVATION: Physical manifestation of TRIANGLE, CIRCLE, SQUARE: Initiation, triangle; Convergence, square (lower body) circle (upper body); Culmination, triangle. Manifestation of *In - Yo*. Mental image: *Yo*.

SHOMENUCHI KOKYU-NAGE

1

Uke utilizes overhead strike from *Gyaku-Hanmi* (photo #1).

APPLIED PRINCIPLES: Stepping forward and to the outside as *Uke* steps in with attack, *Nage* deflects blow with right hand while grasping nape of neck with left hand (photo #2).

2

3

4

Throwing right leg back, *Nage* cuts *Uke's* balance to right rear corner, drawing *Uke* around 180 degrees (photo #3). Driving right palm up and under *Uke's* chin, *Nage* pivots hips sharply back toward *Uke* and applies throw (photos #4 #5).

5

TSUKI KOTEGAESHI

1

3

5

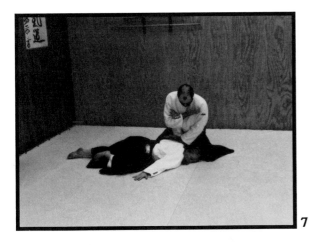

7

Uke utilizes thrusting attack from *Gyaku-Hanmi* (photo #1).

APPLIED PRINCIPLES: Stepping forward and to the outside with right leg as *Uke* steps in with attack, *Nage* deflects blow with right hand while throwing left leg back, drawing *Nage* around 180 degrees (photos #2 #3).

2

4

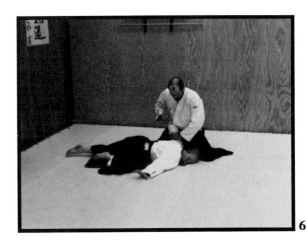

6

Throwing right leg back, *Nage* performs *Kotegaeshi* (photo #4). See *Kotegaeshi, Tachi Waza* (standing technique) section. Moving left hand to *Uke's* inner elbow, *Nage* takes a gliding step forward with right leg, turning and pinning *Uke* to mat (photos #5 #6 #7). See *Katame Waza* section.

TSUKI KAITEN-NAGE

1

2

Uke utilizes thrusting attack from *Ai-Hanmi* (photo #1).

APPLIED PRINCIPLES: Gliding forward and to the outside as *Uke* steps in to strike, *Nage* deflects *Uke's* arm downward with right hand (photo #2).

3

Rotating arm behind, up, and over *Uke's* back, *Nage* suppresses *Uke's* head with left hand while pivoting hips to align with direction of initial attack (photo #3).

4

5

Extending right arm fully, *Nage* rotates hips powerfully toward *Uke*, projecting *Uke's* arm between head and opposite shoulder, followed by a deep step forward with right leg (photos #4 #5).

RYOTETORI KOTEGAESHI *OYO WAZA*

1

Uke utilizes two wrist grab (photo #1).

APPLIED PRINCIPLES: Taking a step directly to the right with right knee, *Nage* raises both arms with strong *Kokyu* power while taking the back of *Uke's* left hand in *Gyaku* (opposite/reverse) *Kotegaeshi* grip (photo #2).

2

3

4

5

Freeing right hand from *Uke's* weakened grip, *Nage* supports *Kotegaeshi* grip with right *Tegatana* while executing throw to *Uke's* left side (photo #3). Gripping *Uke's* wrist with right hand while moving left hand to control inside of elbow, *Nage* takes a deep step forward with right knee implementing turnover (photo #4). Drawing in left knee, *Nage* applies pin (photo #5). See *Katame Waza* section.

HENKA WAZA
(VARIED TECHNIQUES)

KAESHI WAZA
(COUNTER TECHNIQUES)

JIYU/RANDORI WAZA
(FREE STYLE / VARIED ATTACK)

The first portion of this section deals with *Henka Waza*. Literally translated as "varied technique," *Henka Waza* refers to a form of practice in which *Nage* moves freely from one technique to the next, adjusting to the response of *Uke's* body. *Henka Waza* affords *Nage* the opportunity to delve deeper into the physical and spiritual principles of maintaining the "current within the flow." In the performance of *Henka Waza* the applied technique may change one, two, or more times prior to the final application. The second portion of this section deals with *Kaeshi Waza*. Translated within the context of *Aikido* as "counter technique," *Kaeshi Waza* refers to countering action taken by *Uke* at the point of a detected weakness in *Nage's* application of a given technique. *Kaeshi Waza* should be approached as a medium for *Nage's* continued advancement, not as a vehicle for *Uke's* retaliation. Serious note must be taken here, since *Kaeshi Waza* can be both one of the most effective modes of advanced training and one of the most destructive. The negativeness of this problem seems to be seated in the area of the human ego; *Kaeshi Waza* can not be allowed to deteriorate into a contest for the domination of one's will. Possibly within this duality can be found the reason that *O'Sensei* taught only a small group of *Uchi-Deshi* (inside students) the basis for *Kaeshi Waza*, and why so few of these *Waza* have survived intact today. The third and final portion of this section deals with *Jiyu/Randori Waza* as *Taninsu-Geiko* (practice with multiple *Uke*). Translated within the body of *Aikido* as "free style and varied attack," *Jiyu/Randori Waza* serve as intermediate and advanced levels of training which enhance the mind's ability to move freely from one situation to another without being held within the grip of unnecessary encounter. "Deal with one as though with many, deal with many as though with one," this quote of *O'Sensei* deserves serious introspective study on the part of each and every *Aiki-Deshi*. *Henka Waza*, *Kaeshi Waza*, and *Jiyu/Randori Waza* can only be fully comprehended and put to use through a clear understanding of *Kihon Waza*, brought about through disciplined adherence to basic technique.

HENKA WAZA *IKKYO, KOKYU/KOSHI-NAGE, KOTEGAESHI*

1

2

3

Uke utilizes a two hand on one wrist hold from *Gyaku-Hanmi* (photo #1).

APPLIED PRINCIPLES: Gliding to the outside while lowering hips, *Nage* collects *Uke's* energy (photo #2). Throwing left foot back 180 degrees, *Nage* draws *Uke* around, extending right hand toward *Uke* to perform *Ikkyo* (photo #3).

4

5

Moving past *Ikkyo*, *Nage* drives left arm beneath *Uke's* arms while stepping forward deeply with left foot to perform *Kokyu/Koshi-Nage* (photo #4).
Continuing beyond *Kokyu/Koshi-Nage*, *Nage* lowers and rotates hip clockwise while gliding back and beneath *Uke's* arms (photo #5). Sliding to the side with right foot, *Nage* cuts in an arc (down to up) with right hand while taking hold of *Uke's* right wrist (photo #6). Throwing left foot back, *Nage* implements *Kotegaeshi* (photo #7).

6

7

HENKA WAZA IKKYO, KOKYU-NAGE, SHIHO-NAGE

1

Uke utilizes overhead strike from *Gyaku-Hanmi* (photo #1).

APPLIED PRINCIPLES: Gliding forward and to the inside, *Nage* blends with and meets *Uke's* attack, turning *Uke* away with the execution of *Ikkyo* cutting action (photos #2 #3).

2

3

4

5

Moving past *Ikkyo*, *Nage* releases the back of *Uke's* elbow then cuts upward to the inside of elbow with right *Tegatana* (handblade) while rotating *Uke's* wrist clockwise toward elbow with left hand (photo #4).

6

7

Throwing right foot back, *Nage* takes position at a 45 degree angle to *Uke's* center while driving *Atemi* to face with left hand to implement *Kokyu-Nage* (photo #5, previous page). Continuing beyond *Kokyu-Nage*, *Nage* draws back hips while cutting downward and taking control of *Uke's* wrist with both hands (photo #6, previous page).

8

9

10

Gliding forward with powerful counterclockwise hip rotation, *Nage* drives *Uke's* arm upward (photo #7). Stepping forward with right foot, *Nage* pivots hips sharply back to *Uke's* center, bringing wrist to back of *Uke's* shoulder (photo #8). Cutting to point just inside of left foot, *Nage* executes *Shiho-Nage* (photos #9 #10).

OBSERVATION: *Henka Waza* is a method through which to further the development of linking thought and action, action and reaction. Thought must be thought without concrete form, flexible enough to blend with and bend with change of action. Reaction must be the response to action, which takes its own form of action. Yet action formed from reaction must be formless and flexible enough to embrace further action-reaction-action manifestations, open to the flow of the unrestricted mind and body, free from the binds of rigid thought. Herein lies the true value as well as the extreme difficulty involved in the practice of *Henka Waza*.

KAESHI WAZA *KOKYU-NAGE, KOSHI-NAGE*

1

Nage (right, photo #1) utilizes two rear wrist grab, starting from side then moving behind *Uke* to secure grip from *Ai-Hanmi* (photos #2 #3).

APPLIED PRINCIPLES: As *Nage* steps behind, *Uke* steps forward with right foot elongating *Nage's* reach for second grip (photo #3).

2

3

5

4

6

7

Raising left hand, *Uke* takes a large step forward with left foot while rotating hips clockwise toward *Nage*, to perform *Kokyu-Nage* (photo #4). Blending with *Uke's* intent, *Nage* tucks and lowers hips while throwing left foot back 180 degrees, positioning foot beneath *Uke's* center (photo #5). Engaging hips fully, *Nage* implements *Koshi-Nage* (photos #6 #7).

KAESHI WAZA KOTEGAESHI, IRIMI-NAGE

Nage (right) utilizes thrusting attack from *Ai-Hanmi* (photo #1).

APPLIED PRINCIPLES: Gliding forward and to the outside, *Uke* deflects attack (photo #2).

Taking *Nage's* wrist with left hand, *Uke* throws right foot back drawing *Nage* around and off balance (photo #3). As *Uke* turns *Nage's* hand out to perform *Kotegaeshi*, *Nage* blends wrist into application while stepping forward and behind *Uke* with left foot, taking firm hold of *Uke's* collar at nape of neck (photos #4 #5). Throwing right foot back, *Nage* draws *Uke* around 180 degrees while driving right arm in a powerful upward spiral, freeing wrist (photo #6). Stepping deeply behind *Uke* with right foot, *Nage* executes *Irimi-Nage* (photo #7).

NOTE: As with a number of *Kaeshi Waza*, this counter is applied at the point of application, in this instance *Kotegaeshi*. Consequently, the development of extremely strong and flexible joints is a must. Attempting this form of counter premature to this development could lead to severe injury.

JIYU/RANDORI WAZA

1

TANINSU-GEIKO
(PRACTICE WITH MULTIPLE UKE)

2

3

5

4

6

CONTINUED

Jiyu/Randori Waza refers to the free practice of techniques, usually performed in the form of *Taninsu-Geiko* (practice with multiple *Uke*). *Jiyu* specifically refers to practice wherein *Uke* may utilize any reasonable attack while *Nage* has the freedom to apply any technique within the realms of safety. *Randori* is most typically used within the body of *Aikido* when referring to a formalized practice in which *Uke* is given a predetermined attack and *Nage* may respond with any reasonable technique; or *Uke* is given the freedom to utilize any attack but *Nage* must respond with a predetermined defense. "Bringing order to chaos" is an interesting though obscure translation of *Randori* which nonetheless carries the true flavor of the term.

Both forms of practice are utilized to bring about the ability to move the mind and body freely from one point to another employing full focused power, without remaining locked within the previous task. Used at the culmination of a promotional examination, *Jiyu Waza* also demonstrates *Nage's* level of stamina and spirit development.

NOTE: *Taninsu-Geiko* should not be thought of solely as a practice to handle more than one aggressor in a street defense situation. Attack by more than one person must be taken as a threat to life, and dealt with in a most severe manner. Only *Waza* (technique) with the properties to inflict immediate disabling effect without the need for prolonged engagement should be utilized in such a serious situation.

BUKI WAZA
(WEAPON TECHNIQUES)

Divided into two parts, this section introduces both the *Ken* (sword) and *Jo* (staff) utilizing the applied principles of *Aiki*. This segment will embrace the usage of *Ken* and *Jo* as a vital part of the *Riai* (three core forms or "three truths") within the traditional practice of *Aikido*. The *Riai* of *Aikido* consist of *Tai-Jutsu* (body arts), *Aiki-Ken*, and *Aiki-Jo*. It cannot be overstated that the disregard of one element would denote weakness within the others. The first portion of this section will deal with the practice of *Aiki-Ken*. Fortifying development while expanding perspectives on training, *Aiki-Ken* and *Aiki-Jo* furnish numerous subtle yet powerful ramifications to our overall progression. Born from the dedication of *O'Sensei* to years of austere training in *Iwama* (*Dojo* and *Aiki-Jinja*), both *Aiki-Ken* and *Aiki-Jo* should not be confused with the arts of *Kenjutsu* and *Jojutsu* respectively. The use of the *Ken* and *Jo* as developed by *O'Sensei* is both unique in its approach and pin-pointed in its application to the *Tai-Jutsu* (body arts) of *Aikido*. The second portion of this section will deal with the practice of *Aiki-Jo*. *Aiki-Jo* can trace its roots to *O'Sensei's* passion for rigorous training with the *Yari* (Japanese spear), but once again it should be noted that *Aiki-Jo* is not a form of *Yarijutsu* but instead an extraordinary multi-faceted integration of staff and body arts. Each *Aiki-Deshi* should exert daily effort with the *Ken* and *Jo*, steadfastly driving toward a fuller comprehension of the vital significance of the *Riai* and its substantial participation in the development of *Aikido*.

NOTE: An entire volume would be necessary to adequately cover the basic elements involved in *Aiki-Ken* and *Aiki-Jo*. Therefore, we wholeheartedly recommend the <u>*Aikido In Training - Buki Waza*</u> Video Series by this Author as additional reference on this subject.

OBSERVATION: A very positive sign has recently emerged among many *Aikido* instructors worldwide: those who once neglected the essential nature of *Ken* and *Jo* training have now begun to rectify (through their own training) this omission.

AIKI-KEN

(AIKI SWORD)

CHUDAN-NO KAMAE

Chudan-No Kamae (middle level stance): start from the basic posture of *Migi Hanmi* (right, T-shaped stance with back foot at 90 degrees). Hold *Ken* directly outward from abdomen with arms held at natural distance from body (arms extended with slight bend in elbow). Focus should be placed firmly forward (not downward) with emphasis on filling the *Ken* with energy. See note below for proper alignment of blade of *Ken* within posture.

CORRECT

INCORRECT

NOTE: Above left photo demonstrates correct alignment of blade in relationship to forward foot and center; blade must draw a line from center outward , at point just inside of forward foot. Above right photo demonstrates improper alignment; blade draws a line outward, directly over forward foot.

JODAN-NO KAMAE

Jodan-No Kamae (upper level stance): Raise *Ken* above head to an angle of 45 degrees, making sure not to allow right hand to go behind head. Open elbows slightly while keeping shoulders down. Concentrate weight in lower body; center of gravity and/or mind must not follow raising motion of *Ken*. *Jodan-No Kamae* may be performed in either *Migi* (right) or *Hidari* (left) *Hanmi*.

GEDAN-NO KAMAE

USHIRO GEDAN-NO KAMAE

Gedan-No Kamae (lower level stance): From *Migi* (right) *Hanmi*, lower *Ken* while turning blade to face left. Position left hand in front of left hip while aligning right hand with center. *Kissaki* (point of blade) is held just to the outside of forward foot (photo at left).

Ushiro Gedan-No Kamae (rear lower level stance): From *Hidari* (left) *Hanmi*, lower *Ken* to the rear while turning blade away from body. Position right hand in front of right hip while aligning left hand with center (photo at right). Posture may also be performed as *Ushiro Chudan* (rear middle level stance).

KEN GRIP

KEN GRIP

Grip *Ken* with right hand forward while keeping left hand closest to body (little finger gripping the last inch of the handle). Leave one grip's distance between hands while aligning webbing of thumb and forefinger with top of blade.

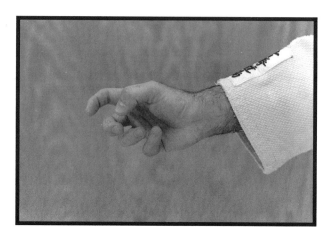

GRIPPING METHOD

First gripping powerfully with little finger, progress forward to ring finger then middle finger. Thumb completes grip by folding down in direction of middle finger. Note: Index finger does not hold, instead upper portion of finger presses inward during grip.

SUBURI: SOLO CUTTING EXERCISE

Ken-No Suburi consists of two sets of seven cutting exercises each. The first set is referred to as the advancing movement set, due primarily to the alternate advancing motion found in the fourth through seventh *Suburi*. The second set is referred to as the lateral movement set, due to its emphasis on movement to both the left and right. *Suburi* represent the basis of all cutting action within the body of *Aiki-Ken*. The *Ken* is always held with a firm live grip, never squeezed or held in a death grip. At the completion of a cut or thrust the *Ken* is gripped in a powerful wringing motion (right hand wrings counterclockwise, left hand wrings clockwise) allowing for the spirit to be extended throughout the *Ken* and beyond. It is important here to note that the movement of the *Ken* as used in *Aikido* is not the same as used in *Kenjutsu* (classical fencing) or *Kendo* its modern sport derivative. *Aiki-Ken* is the practice of the *Ken* endowed with the spirit of *Aiki* and the practice of *Aiki* expressed through the spirit of the *Ken*. *Aiki-Ken* was created solely by *O'Sensei Ueshiba Morihei*; it is a most vital part of the *Riai* (parts embodying a whole art) of *Aikido*.

NOTE: On the following six pages are examples of the advancing movement set of seven *Suburi*. Clarity of purpose, exertion of the spirit, attention to form, and daily repetition should be the focal point of one's endeavor in laying the groundwork for *Aiki-Ken* through the understanding of *Ken-No Suburi*.

KEN-NO SUBURI *BASIC SOLO CUTTING EXERCISES*

DAI-ICHI NO SUBURI: Starting from *Chudan-No Kamae* in *Migi-Hanmi* (photo #1), draw back right foot half the distance to left foot while raising *Ken* above head to the position of *Jodan-No Kamae* (see *Kamae* section). Allowing *Ken* to lower slightly to rear, advance front foot and cut down powerfully with strong forward projection (photos #2 #3 #4).

NOTE: As in all *Suburi*, center must be lowered, hips must be firmly engaged, and *Ken* grip must be applied in a powerful wringing manner at the culmination of the cutting motion.

DAI-NI NO SUBURI: Starting from *Chudan-No Kamae* in *Migi-Hanmi* (photo #1), draw and raise *Ken* to *Jodan-No Kamae* while stepping back with right foot to present an oblique hips posture in *Hidari-Hanmi* (photos #2 #3). Rotating hips firmly counterclockwise, step forward and cut down powerfully with strong forward projection (photos #4 #5).

KEN-NO SUBURI

1

DAI-SAN NO SUBURI: Starting from *Chudan-No Kamae* in *Migi-Hanmi* (photo #1), step back and raise *Ken* as in *Dai-Ni No Suburi* (photo #2). Maintaining oblique hip position, lower *Ken* to *Ushiro Chudan-No Kamae* (photo #3 - #3a, reverse angle).

2

NOTE: The *Ken* may also be positioned directly above the head in the *Misogi Ken* posture of inhaling the breath of the universe (photo #2).

3

3a

4

5

6

Leading upward in one smooth arcing motion, starting at the left elbow, raise the *Ken* above the head to *Jodan-No Kamae* (photo #4). Rotating hips firmly counterclockwise, step forward and cut down powerfully with strong forward projection (photos #5 #6).

1

2

3

4

5

6

7

DAI-YON NO SUBURI: Starting from *Chudan-No Kamae* in *Migi-Hanmi* (photo #1), perform *Dai-Ichi No Suburi* (photos #2 #3 #4). Continue by stepping forward and slightly off line with left foot while raising *Ken* in a straight line to a position above head (photo #5). Bringing right foot up, engage hips and cut down powerfully with strong forward projection (photos #6 #7). Raising *Ken* step forward with right foot and execute right side cut in the same manner (photos #8 #9 #10).

8

9

10

KEN-NO SUBURI

1

2

3

4

DAI-GO NO SUBURI: Starting from *Chudan-No Kamae* in *Migi-Hanmi* (photo #1), raise *Ken* keeping blade to right and step forward and slightly off line with left foot while bringing body beneath *Ken* (photo #2). Drawing right foot up and onto line with left foot, rotate *Ken* counterclockwise to position above head and cut down powerfully while engaging hips (photos #3 #4). Raise *Ken* keeping blade to left and step forward with right foot while rotating *Ken* clockwise above head and execute cut in the same manner (photos #5 #6 #7 #8).

5

6

NOTE: When raising *Ken*, body must be brought forward beneath *Ken* (photos #2 #5), *Ken* must not be drawn back to be brought above head.

7

8

1

2

3

4

5

6

DAI-ROKU NO SUBURI: Starting from *Chudan-No Kamae* in *Migi-Hanmi* (photo #1), raise *Ken* keeping blade to right and step forward with left foot executing downward cut in the same manner as *Dai-Go No Suburi* (photos #2 #3 #4 #5). At completion of cut, glide left foot forward slightly while rotating blade counterclockwise (to horizontal) and execute thrust to the level of the solar plexus (photo #6). Raise *Ken* keeping blade to left, step forward with right foot and execute downward cut (photos #7 #8 #9 #10). Glide right foot forward slightly while rotating blade clockwise (to horizontal) and execute thrust (photo #11).

7

8

9

10

11

307

KEN-NO SUBURI

DAI-SHICHI NO SUBURI: Starting from *Chudan-No Kamae* in *Migi-Hanmi* (photo #1), raise *Ken* above head while stepping back with right foot and oblique hips (photo #2). Rotating hips powerfully counterclockwise, step forward with right foot and execute downward cut in the same manner as *Dai-Ni No Suburi* (photos #3 #4 #5). Rotating hips clockwise step forward with left foot and execute powerful thrust to the level of the solar plexus (photos #6 #7).

NOTE: When executing thrust *Ken* must be kept forward of the body (photos #6 #7). Body should not pass the gripped portion of the *Ken* and arms must not be used in an excessive pumping manner.

TANREN-UCHI *FORGING THE SPIRIT*

The Japanese word *Tanren* translates to mean "forging the spirit." *Uchi* translated means "strike," therefore *Tanren-Uchi* is said to mean "the forging of the spirit through repetitious striking." Performed with a heavy bladed *Ken* referred to as a *Tanren Ken*, this form of striking exercise is not only valuable in training the spirit, but also is an aid in the physical development of the muscles of the lower back as well as the forearms and wrists. Performed on a tire mounted at the height of about three and one half feet, the *Deshi* (student) attempts to suppress the recoil of full power strikes. To add to the severity of this, the *Ken* is held in a closed hand *Ken* grip (see close-up) with heel of right hand in line with webbing (between thumb and index finger) of left hand. *Tanren-Uchi* may be performed either solo or paired (shown). Basic strikes are performed utilizing *Dai-Ichi No Ken Suburi* with the addition of lowering the *Ken* to a position fully behind the back and in line with the spine.

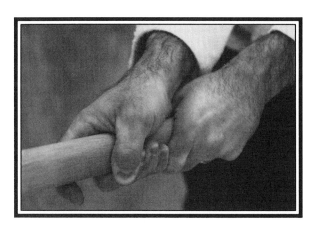

PAIRED *TANREN-UCHI* PRACTICE: As the *Ken* on the right is raised, the *Ken* on the left is on its path downward (photo #1). As the *Ken* on the left makes contact, the *Ken* on the right is just reaching the back portion of its swing in preparation to strike forward (photo #2). When the *Ken* on the left reaches full impact, the *Ken* on the right has begun its forward cutting motion (photo #3).

KUMI *PAIRED INTERACTIVE MOVEMENTS*

Basic *Kumi* interactions consist of the following: the twelve *Kumi Ken*, one of which (*Dai-Go No Kumi Ken*) is demonstrated in this section; the six *Kumi Tachi* which includes *Ki Musubi-No Tachi* (tying of *Ki*); and five *Futari-No Kumi Ken* (*Kumi* with two attacking partners), two of which (*Dai-Ni No* and *Dai-San No Futari-No Kumi Ken*) are also demonstrated in this section. *Kumi* practice presents us with many ways through which to learn the various aspects of blending, distancing, entering, and withdrawing as well as rapid hip shifting and reading and exploiting openings in our partners' attacks. Initial training starts with open distance and no contact. After sufficient understanding has been developed, training moves to actual distance with light contact at medium speed. Advanced practice consists of heavy contact (*Ken* to *Ken*) performed at full speed. It is important to note that for *Kumi* to be performed productively and safely it must follow this natural progression. Even those with a high level of skill must keep this progression in mind and begin with light contact during each *Keiko* (training). Partners are designated as *Uke-Ken* (receiving sword) and *Uchi-Ken* (attacking sword); *Uke-Ken* always perseveres. Each basic *Kumi Ken/Tachi* has one or more secondary variations. One year of dedicated *Suburi* practice is the prerequisite before exploring *Kumi Ken* training.

KUMI KEN

1

DAI-GO NO KUMI KEN: Starting from *Kissaki-Ma* (middle level with tips of *Ken* touching), *Uchi* (left) begins to raise *Ken* to strike. Simultaneously *Uke* (right) glides forward driving back *Uchi's Ken* (photos #1 #2).

2

3

4

Uchi responds by moving behind to strike at back of *Uke's* right leg (photo #3), *Uke* matches movement to block attack (photo #4).

5

Uchi (now right) lifts *Ken* and steps forward with thrust to *Uke's* chest. *Uke* (now left) responds by stepping back deflecting *Uchi's Ken* to left (photos #5 #6).

6

7

8

As *Uchi* raises *Ken* and steps forward to deliver strike to *Uke's* neck, *Uke* steps forward riding movement of *Uchi's Ken* while moving to *Uchi's* right and delivers strike to wrist as *Uchi* completes attack (photos #7 #8 #9).

9

FUTARI-NO KUMI KEN KUMI WITH TWO PARTNERS

1

Dai-Ni No Futari-No Kumi Ken: From *Chudan-No Kamae* (middle level), both *Uchi* (left and right) raise *Ken* and glide forward to perform overhead cut. Moving to the outside, *Uke* (center) delivers cut across chest of forward *Uchi* (photos #1 #2).

2

3

4

5

Completing cut with second step, *Uke* pivots and matches cut to center (photos #3 #4). Turning attack to *Uke's* new position, both *Uchi* again utilize overhead strike. Stepping at an angle away from *Uchi* on left, *Uke* throws left leg back 90 degrees and delivers cut to head of *Uchi* on right (photos #5 #6).

6

1

Dai-San No Futari-No Kumi Ken: From *Chudan-No Kamae*, both *Uchi* (left and right) raise *Ken* and glide forward to perform overhead cut. Throwing right leg back 225 degrees, *Uke* (center) turns and delivers cut across chest of *Uchi* to rear (photos #1 #2 #3).

2

3

4

5

Taking a step forward with left foot as *Uchi* (right) commences attack to *Uke's* new position, *Uke* pivots and offsets slightly to right while delivering cut to *Uchi's* head (photos #4 #5 #6).

6

AIKI-JO

(AIKI STAFF)

JO-NO KAMAE BASIC POSTURES OF AIKI-JO

KIHON-NO JO KAMAE

Kihon-No Jo Kamae (basic beginning stance): From *Hidari-Hanmi* (left, T-shaped stance with back foot at 90 degrees), hold *Jo* in left hand while placing bottom end on mat no more than six inches forward of left foot. Holding the *Jo* two to six inches from the top end, incline *Jo* forward slightly. Posture should encase *Deshi* within a triangle with the *Jo* being centered to the forefront, much like the bow of a boat. The *Jo* should be held firmly but not rigidly. *Kihon-No Jo Kamae* is the basic starting position for many *Aiki-Jo* movements and allows for rapid striking and blocking motions in virtually any direction.

TSUKI-NO KAMAE

Tsuki-No Kamae (thrust ready stance): From *Hidari-Hanmi*, in a slightly wider than normal stance, position the *Jo* facing forward with the right hand holding the back end of the *Jo* directly in front of the area of the navel while the left hand holds slightly forward of mid *Jo*. Hips should be kept in a low position while right hand holds tightly and left hand holds firmly yet not rigidly. *Tsuki-No Kamae* may also be performed with the forward hand in a reversed holding manner (thumb to the inside). A form of *Chudan-No Kamae*, *Tsuki-No Kamae* places the *Deshi* in a *Tsuki* (thrusting) ready stance.

316

CHUDAN-NO KAMAE

Chudan-No Kamae (middle level stance): From *Migi-Hanmi* (right posture), hold *Jo* directly forward on a level plane (photo at left). Right hand should be extended forward of center while left hand is in line with left hip, and forward end of *Jo* is aligned with right hip. Hands should be placed two to two and one half grips apart, with left hand gripping tightly and right hand utilizing a firm but not rigid grip.

JODAN-NO KAMAE

Jodan-No Kamae (upper level stance): From *Hidari-Hanmi*, raise *Jo* above head at a 45 degree angle (photo at right). Left hand is extended slightly forward of forehead and holds tightly while right hand is held directly above head with a firm yet not rigid grip. Sight is directed between arms; care should be taken not to open elbows excessively.

USHIRO GEDAN-NO KAMAE

Ushiro Gedan-No Kamae (rear lower level stance): From *Hidari-Hanmi*, thrust *Jo* to rear while assuming a lower and wider than normal posture (photo at left). Left hand is held forward of abdomen while right hand is positioned on line drawn back at 45 degrees from right foot. Left hand has tight grip while right hand has firm but not rigid grip.

NOTE: *Tsuki, Chudan, Jodan,* and *Gedan-No Kamae* as well as all *Jo* postures and movements may be performed in either *Migi* or *Hidari-Hanmi* with either right or left hand forward.

317

JO-NO KAMAE

HASSO-NO KAMAE

Hasso-No Kamae (shoulder level stance): From *Hidari-Hanmi* raise *Jo* to vertical position in line with right hip and shoulder. Hand holding the base of the *Jo* always faces toward body, but hand held one forearm distance from base may face away (loaded position, shown) or toward body (unloaded position).

NOTE: *Hasso-No Kamae* may be performed in either *Hidari* (shown) or *Migi-Hanmi*. When performed in *Migi-Hanmi Jo* is positioned at 45 degree angle to rear with lowermost hand held six to twelve inches from base of *Jo*.

JODAN-NO UKE-DOME

Jodan-No Uke-Dome (upper level receiving stance): From *Hidari-Hanmi*, raise *Jo* to blocking position directly above head. Back hand is kept slightly higher than front hand and hands are positioned to front and rear of head. *Jo* is always held with palm of rear hand facing away from body, but forward hand may be held facing away (shown) or toward body.

NOTE: *Jodan-No Uke-Dome* may be performed in either *Hidari* (shown) or *Migi-Hanmi*.

SUBURI: SOLO EXERCISE

Jo-No Suburi consists of twenty individual exercises which constitute the basic usage of the *Aiki-Jo*. Each *Suburi*, once learned, can be applied at various levels, angles, and in virtually any direction. Endowed with the unique quality of having infinite edges as well as the capability of either end being utilized, the *Jo* also requires the development of rapid hand dexterity. As with *Ken*, the *Jo* is held with a firm live grip, never squeezed in a death grip. Unlike *Ken* the *Jo* allows for the movement of the hands along its entire length. One hand is utilized as the hard hand (firm grip) while the other is used as the soft hand (fluid grip), both being applied with a powerful wringing motion (right hand wrings counterclockwise, left hand wrings clockwise) at the completion of each thrust, cut, or blocking movement. A highly important aspect shared by both the *Ken* and *Jo* is the necessity of aligning the final striking posture with the ball of the backmost foot, allowing for full and proper engagement of the hips. On the following four pages are examples of ten of the most significant *Suburi*. Created by *O'Sensei* as a vital element of the *Riai* of Aikido, rigorous endeavor in *Jo-No Suburi* is required as the foundation of training in *Aiki-Jo*.

JO-NO SUBURI

1 **2** **3**

CHOKU TSUKI: Starting from *Kihon-No Jo Kamae* (photo #1), raise *Jo* into *Tsuki-No Kamae* (photos #2 #3), gliding forward execute mid-level thrust (photo #4).

TSUKI GEDAN GAESHI: As an extension of *Choku Tsuki*, pull *Jo* fully to rear while gliding slightly back (photo #5A). Stepping forward with right foot execute low level strike (photos #6A #7A).

4

TSUKI JODAN GAESHI: Also an extension of *Choku Tsuki*, raise *Jo* above head while gliding back slightly and moving left foot to the right (photo #5B). Releasing left hand rotate *Jo* clockwise above head, grasp end of *Jo* with left hand step forward executing downward strike (photos #6B #7B).

5a **5b**

6a **6b**

7a **7b**

JO-NO SUBURI

1

2

3

4

KATATE GEDAN GAESHI: Execute *Choku Tsuki* (photo #1), glide slightly back drawing *Jo* to rear while bringing hands tightly together (photo #2). Step forward with right foot executing wide circular movement from low to high with right hand, stopping *Jo* above and behind head with left hand (photos #3 #4).

1

2

3

HASSO GAESHI UCHI: From *Chudan-No Kamac* (photo #1), glide left foot slightly back while drawing *Jo* with left hand (photo #2). Step back with right foot while bringing right hand to hip and left hand to right side of head (photo #3). Driving *Jo* forward and down in tight rotation, release left hand and spin *Jo* into an upright position at right shoulder (photo #4). Reversing right hand hold while shifting weight forward step in with right foot and execute downward strike (photos #5 #6).

4

5

6

 1

 2

KAESHI TSUKI: From *Kihon-No Jo Kamae* (photo #1), advance left foot and slide left hand down *Jo* while grasping upper end of *Jo* with right hand in a reverse (thumb down) manner (photo #2). Bringing *Jo* to *Tsuki-No Kamae*, execute mid-level thrust (photos #3 #4).

 3

 4

 1

 2

SHOMEN UCHIKOMI: From *Chudan-No Kamae* (photo #1), step back with right foot while raising *Jo* above head and obliquing hips (photo #2). Shifting weight suddenly forward, step in with right foot executing downward strike (photos #3 #4).

 3

 4

RENZOKU UCHIKOMI: An extension of *Shomen Uchikomi*, raise *Jo* above head while shifting weight forward (photo #5A). Rotating *Jo* counterclockwise above head step forward with left foot executing downward strike (photos #6A #7A).

 5a

 6a

 7a

JO-NO SUBURI

1

2

3

4

MIGI NAGARE GAESHI TSUKI: From *Chudan-No Kamac* (photo #1), raise and turn *Jo* counterclockwise above head while stepping forward with left foot and execute downward strike (photos #2 #3). Shifting weight to left foot, move left hand forward to center of *Jo* (photo #4). Throw back right foot 180 degrees raising *Jo* to *Jodan-No Ukc-Dome* (photo #5). Bringing *Jo* down in a sharp circular motion with right hand, execute *Choku Tsuki* (photos #6 #7).

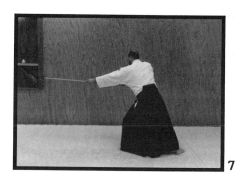

5

6

7

USHIRO TSUKI: From *Kihon-No Jo Kamac* (photo #1), simultaneously draw left foot back and grasp upper end of *Jo* with right hand while raising *Jo* tightly against left forearm (photo #2). Continuing rearward step with left foot execute thrusting strike to the rear while retaining forward facing *Hanmi* (photo #3).

1

2

3

KUMI *PAIRED INTERACTIVE MOVEMENTS*

Basic *Kumi* (paired movements) interactions consist of the following: the ten *Kumi Jo*; the five *Kumi-Kata* (*Kata* or solo extended movements, which when split and paired become *Kumi* in and of themselves), one of which (*Dai-Ni No Kumi-Kata*) appears in this section; the five *Kumi Jo-No Ken* (staff to sword *Kumi*), one of which (*Dai-Ni No Kumi Jo-No Ken*) appears in this section. Also part of the body of *Aiki-Jo* training are the three *Gyaku* (opposing) *Kata*, which when paired with the three basic *Kata* (solo performed multiple movement series) are transformed into extended *Kumi* interactions. The uniqueness of *Jo* training exists in the ability to use any surface as well as either end as a strike zone while at the same time allowing for a wide variety of hand positioning. Embodied with the ability to be turned and rotated, the pivotal point of the *Jo* may be moved up or down its length, giving us an insight into applied movement, force, and usage of opposite and aligned energies. Large circular motion mixed with subtle hip and postural movement as well as rapid hand changes, help to open various levels of understanding often paralleling those of *Kumi Ken* (see *Ken* section). As with *Ken*, one year of *Suburi* is the standard prerequisite for beginning *Kumi* training.

KUMI-KATA

1

DAI-NI NO KUMI-KATA: Starting from *Migi Hanmi* in *Chudan-No Kamae*, *Uke* (left) glides back drawing *Jo* to rear as *Uchi* (right) delivers a thrusting attack (photos #1 #2 #3).

2

3

4

Raising *Jo* above head, *Uke* steps forward with left foot and delivers strike toward *Uchi's* head. *Uchi* responds by lifting front end of *Jo* to meet and deflect *Uke's* downward movement (photos #4 & #5-next page).

KUMI-KATA

5

6

Changing ends of *Jo*, *Uke* strikes top of *Uchi's Jo* as *Uchi* attacks with thrust (photos #6 #7). *Uke* utilizes thrust to *Uchi's* ribcage (photo #8).

7

8

9

10

11

12

Sliding *Jo* to other end, *Uchi* deflects attack while changing *Hanmi* (photo #9). Lifting rear of *Jo*, *Uchi* delivers downward thrusting attack as *Uke* slides to side blocking with *Jodan-No Uke-Dome* (photos #10 #11).

13

Turning *Jo* above head while changing hands, *Uke* delivers downward strike to *Uchi's* knee. Gliding back, *Uchi* lowers *Jo* to execute block (photos #12-previous page & #13). Changing to *Hidari-Hanmi* and moving back to centerline, *Uke* spins *Jo* into *Hasso-No Kamae* while *Uchi* rotates back end of *Jo* forward assuming *Chudan-No Kamae* (photos #14 #15 #16).

14

15

16

17

As *Uchi* commits fully to a thrusting attack, *Uke* steps deeply to the outside with right foot, draws left foot onto line with *Uchi's* center and delivers finishing downward thrust to sternum area (photos #17 #18).

NOTE: A distinguishing feature of all five *Kumi-Kata* is that both *Uke* and *Uchi* draw back into solid *Kamae* just prior to final interaction.

18

KUMI JO-NO KEN *PAIRED - STAFF TO SWORD*

1

DAI-NI NO KUMI JO-NO KEN: *Ukc* (*Jo*) moves to right deflecting *Uchi's* (*Ken*) initial thrust. *Uchi* then advances with cut toward neck as *Uke* moves left deflecting attack and drawing into *Hasso-No Kamac* (photos #1 #2 #3 #4 #5 #6).

2

3

4

5

6

7

Stepping with right foot, *Uchi* delivers overhead strike. Moving right, *Ukc* responds with final downward strike to *Uchi's* temple (photos #7 #8).

8

JO-NAGE *THROWING BY STAFF*

Jo-Nage differs from *Jo-Dori* (staff taking, see final page *Shiho-Nage* section) in that *Nage* invites *Uke* to take the *Jo* then follows with a throw, rather than *Uke* having first wielded the *Jo*. The practice of *Jo-Nage* promotes proper timing as well as the development of *Kokyu* extension beyond the physical body.

KOKYU WAZA : *Nage* invites *Uke's* grasp from *Chudan-No Kamae* (photo #1). At point of *Uke's* grasp, *Nage* drives *Jo* across *Uke's* center and beneath arm while taking a large gliding step forward to implement throw (photos #2 #3). As *Uke* rises, *Nage* pulls *Jo* to rear then steps forward to invite *Uke's* grasp. At point *Uke* commits to attack, *Nage* directs *Jo* over *Uke's* head sweeping back of knee to execute throw (photos #4 #5 #6 #7).

GLOSSARY

Agatsu - Self-victory, victory over self.

Ai - Harmony, to be in harmony with.

Ai-Hanmi - Partners in mutual stance.

Aiki - Harmonious energy/spirit.

Aiki-Budo - Early name of *Aikido*.

Aiki-Deshi - Student of *Aikido*.

Aikido - Way of spiritual harmony.

Aikidoka - Practitioner of *Aikido*, one of high rank.

Aiki-En - *Aiki* farm, early name of *Iwama Dojo* site.

Aiki-Jinja - *Aiki* shrine, located next to *Iwama Dojo*.

Aiki-Jo - *Aiki* staff.

Aikikai Hombu Dojo - Post-war name of *Kobukan Dojo*.

Aiki-Ken - *Aiki* sword.

Aiki-Nage - *Aiki* throw.

Aiki-Otoshi - *Aiki* drop.

Atemi - Strike, primarily to create response.

Ate Waza - Striking technique.

Awase - Blending.

Ayabe - Site of *Omoto-Kyo Shinto* sect Hdqt.

Bu - Martial.

Budo - Martial Way.

Budo - Second of two books by *O'Sensei*.

Budo Renshu - First of two books by *O'Sensei*.

Bujutsu - Martial art/science.

Buki Waza - Weapon techniques.

Bushi - Warrior or warrior caste.

Chudan - Middle level.

Chudan Giri - Middle level cut.

Chudan-no Kamae - Middle level stance.

Chudan Tsuki - Middle level thrust.

Chushin - Centerline.

Daito-Ryu Jujutsu - Martial art of *Takeda Sokaku*.

Dan - Black belt level rank.

Deguchi Nao - Founder of *Omoto-Kyo Shinto* sect.

Deguchi Onisaburo - Successor to *Deguchi Nao*.

Deshi - Student.

Do - Way/path.

Dojo - Way place, training place of the Way.

Dojo-Cho - Chief instructor of *Dojo*.

Doka - Poems of the Way, long form poems.

Doshu - Way leader.

Doto - System of family succession.

Eritori - Grasping the nape of the collar.

Eritori Shomenuchi - Nape of collar hold with strike.

Futari - Two persons.

Futari-no Kumi Jo/Ken - *Kumi* with two attackers.

Gaeshi - Turn/twist.

Gambatte - Persevere/overcome hardship.

Ganseki-Otoshi - Heels over head drop.

Gedan - Lower level.

Gedan-no Kamae - Low level stance.

Geri - Kick.

Giri - Cut, also spelled *Kiri*.

Go - Five.

Gokyo - Fifth teaching.

Gyaku - Reversed/opposite.

Gyaku-Hanmi - Partners in opposite stance.

Gyaku Ryokatatori/Munadori - Grasping opposite lapels.

Hakama - Uniform, traditional pleated pants.

Hana Koshi-Nage - Popping/recoiling hip throw.

Hanmi - T-shaped stance with back foot at 90 degrees.

Hanmi Handachi - Half-body/Half-standing.

Hantai - Cross hand grab.

Hara - Center.

Hasso-no Kamae - Shoulder level stance (weapon).

Henka Waza - Varied techniques.

Hidari - Left.

Hidari-Hanmi - Left T-shaped stance.

Hiji - Elbow.

Hiji-Kime - Elbow focus.

Hiji-Nage - Elbow throw.

Hiji-Tori - Elbow grab.

Hiji Waza - Elbow technique.

Ichi - One.

Ikkyo - First teaching.

In-Yo - Negative-Positive Female-Male etc.

Inoue Noriaki - Nephew of *O'Sensei*.

Irimi - Enter/entering/enter into.

Irimi-Nage - Entering throw.

Iwama Dojo - *Ibaragi* Prefecture *Dojo* of *O'Sensei*.

Jiyu Waza - Freestyle technique.

Jo - Staff.

Jodan - Upper level.

Jodan-no Kamae - Upper level stance.

Jo-Dori - Staff taking.

Jo-Nage - Throwing with staff.

Juji-Garami - Cross entwining.

Juji-Nage - Cross throw.

Jumbi Taiso - Preparatory exercises.

Kaeshi Waza - Reversed/counter technique.

Kagami-Biraki - New Year's celebration.

Kaiten-Nage - Rotary throw.

Kamae - Stance.

Kamiza - Upper seat, focal point at head of training area.

Kata - Lapel/shoulder area.

Kata - Formal practice of preset forms.

Katame Waza - Techniques of immobilization.

Katatetori - One wrist grab.

Katatori/Munadori - Lapel/shoulder grab.

Katsuhayabi - Moment of swift victory.

Katsujinken - Life giving sword.

Keiko - Reflecting on times past, training.

Keiko-Dogi - Training uniform of the Way.

Ken - Sword.

Ken-no Awase - Blending with sword.

Ken-no Kamae - Beginning stance of sword movements.

Ken-no Suburi - Solo cutting exercise with sword.

Ken no Tai-Sabaki - Evasive body movement with sword.

Ken-Tori - Sword taking.

Ki - Energy/life-force/spirit.

Kiai - Shout of *Ki* rushing forth.

Kihaku - Projecting beyond the physical body.

Kihon - Foundation/basic.

Kihon Geiko - Foundation training, beginners practice.

Kihon Waza - Basic techniques.

Kime - Focus.

Ki-no Musubi - Tying of *Ki*.

Ki-no Nagare - *Ki* flow.

Kiri - Cut, also spelled *Giri*.

Kiri-no Ken - Repetitious cutting with *Ken*.

Kissaki Ma - Distance at which tips of swords touch.

Kobukan - Pre-war name of *Aikikai Hombu Dojo*.

Kogeki - Terms of attacks.

Kohai - Junior level student.

Kojiki - Records of ancient matters.

Kokoro - Heart, fortitude of the spirit.

Kokyu - Breath.

Kokyu-Dosa - Breath exercise.

Kokyu-Ho - Breath exercise method.

Kokyu-Nage - Breath throw.

Kokyu Ryoku - Breath power.

Kokyu Ryoku Taiso - Breath power exercise.

Koshi - Hip.

Koshi-Nage - Hip throw.

Kote - Wrist.

Kotegaeshi - Wrist turn.

Kubishime - Strangle.

Kumi - Paired interactive weapon movements.

Kumi Jo-no Ken - Staff to sword interactions.

Kumi-Kata - Series of movements solo or with partner.

Kumi Ken/Kumi Tachi - Interactive sword movements.

Kyu - Lower levels in ranking system.

Maai - Proper distance.

Mae-Geri - Front kick.

Mae Tori - Front grappling attack.

Mae Ukemi - Front roll.

Masakatsu - Correct victory.

Men - head.

Men-Nage - Head throw.

Menuchi - Head strike.

Michi - Path.

Migi - Right.

Migi-Hanmi - Right T-shaped stance.

Misogi - Purifying the body and spirit.

Misogi Ken - Inhaling the breath of the universe.

Mudansha - Below *Dan* rank.

Musubi - Tying/knot.

Nagare - Flow/flowing.

Nage - Throw/thrower.

Nage Waza - Throwing technique.

Nen - Centered in thought, deed, and moment.

Ni - Two.

Nikyo - Second teaching.

Omote - Front, area to the front.

Omoto-Kyo - Great origin, sect of *Shinto*.

O'Sensei - One who has gone a great distance before, title
        given Founder of *Aikido, Ueshiba Morihei.*

Otoshi - Drop.

Oyo - Varied/applied.

Randori - Formalized varied attack/practice.

Rei - Bow.

Reigi - Etiquette.

Renshu - Practice/drill.

Riai - Core forms of an art.

Ritsu-Rei - Standing Bow.

Ryokatatori - Two lapel grab.

Ryoku - Power.

Ryote - Two hands.

Ryotemochi - Two hands on one arm hold.

Ryotetori - Two hand grab, one on one.

Ryu - Style/school.

Sabaki - Evasive movement.

San - Three.

Sankyo - Third teaching.

Satori - Enlightenment.

Satsujinken - Life taking sword.

Seika-Tanden - Center, one-point.

Seiza - Formal seated posture.

Sempai - Senior level student.

Sen-no-Sen - Seizing the initiative.

Sensei - One who has gone before, teacher.

Shiho-Nage - Four direction throw.

Shikko - Knee-walking.

Shinken - Live sword.

Shinto - Native religion of Japan.

Shisei - Posture.

Shomen - Front/head of mat.

Shomen Giri - Downward cut to the head.

Shomenuchi - Overhead strike.

Shoshin - Beginners mind.

Shoshinsha - Beginner.

Shoza - Front seat.

Shugyo - Austere training.

Shugyosha - One dedicated to *Shugyo*.

Soto - Outside.

Soto-Tegatana - Outside handblade.

Suburi - Solo cutting exercise.

Suigetsu - Moon on water, drawing reflective reaction.

Suigetsu - Area of the solar-plexus.

Suki - Opening.

Sumi-Otoshi - Corner drop.

Suwari Waza - Seated techniques.

Tachi - Standing.

Tachi - Sword.

Tachi-Dori - Sword taking.

Tachi Waza - Standing techniques.

Tai-Jutsu - Body arts.

Tai-no Henko - Body changing/shifting.

Tai-Sabaki - Evasive body turning.

Taiso - Exercise.

Takeda Sokaku - Headmaster *Daito-Ryu Jujutsu*.

Takemusu - Spontaneous creation.

Tanabe - Birthplace of *O'Sensei*.

Taninsu-Geiko - Practice with multiple *Uke*.

Tanren - Forging the spirit.

Tanren Ken - Heavy bladed *Ken*.

Tanto - Knife.

Tanto-Tori - Knife taking.

Tegatana - Handblade.

Tenchi - Heaven and earth.

Tenchi-Nage - Heaven and earth throw.

Tenkan - Turning/turning off of.

Tetsubo - Circuit of energy.

Tokonoma - Alcove.

Toma - Partners at two step distance.

Tsuki - Thrusting attack.

Tsuki-no Kamae - Thrust ready stance.

Uchi - Strike.

Uchi - Inside.

Uchi-Deshi - Inside student.

Uchi-Jo - Attacking *Jo*.

Uchi-Ken - Attacking *Ken*.

Uchi-Tegatana - Inside handblade.

Ueshiba Hatsu - Spouse of *O'Sensei*.

Ueshiba Juku - Name of *O'Sensei's* first *Dojo*.

Ueshiba Kisshomaru - Son of *O'Sensei*, current *Doshu*.

Ueshiba Morihei - *O'Sensei*, Founder of *Aikido*.

Ueshiba Moriteru - Grandson of *O'Sensei*, current *Waka*.

Ueshiba Yoroku - Father of *O'Sensei*.

Ueshiba Yuki - Mother of *O'Sensei*.

Uke - Receiver/attacker.

Uke-Dome - Upper level receiving posture.

Uke-Jo - Receiving *Jo*.

Uke-Ken - Receiving *Ken*.

Ukemi - Art of receiving.

Ura - Rear/area to the rear.

Ushiro - Back/behind.

Ushiro Ukemi - Back roll.

Waka - In line to become successor.

Waza - Technique.

Yari - Spear.

Yoko-Geri - Circular kick.

Yonkyo - Fourth teaching.

Yudansha - Of *Dan* rank, black belt level.

Za - Seat.

Zanshin - Lingering/connecting spirit.

Za-Rei - Seated bow.

For more biographical information on the life of *O'Sensei* and the history of *Aikido*
we recommend the following sources:

Aikido Kaiso Ueshiba Morihei Den (Japanese language text - 1977)

Aikido Kaiso: Ueshiba Morihei Seitan Hyakunen (compilation of hundreds of photographs covering the life
of *O'Sensei*, Japanese text with English language supplement - 1983)

above by *Ueshiba Kisshomaru, Aikido Doshu*

Ueshiba Morihei to *Aikido: Kaiso O'Kataru 19 Ninno Deshi Tachi* (a collection of 19 interviews with
personal students of *O'Sensei*, Japanese language text - 1990)

Aikido Masters: Pre-war Students of *Ueshiba Morihei* (collection of 14 interviews, English language - 1992)

The *Aiki*-News Encyclopedia of *Aikido* (English language text - 1991)

Aiki-News (a quarterly publication in Japanese, English, and French language - 1974 to present)

Aiki-News: Video Library (extensive collection of footage of *O'Sensei* and *Aikido,* available through *Aiki*-News)

above by Stanley Pranin, Editor-in-Chief *Aiki*-News

Aikido Kaiso Ueshiba Morihei (Japanese language text - 1969)

above by *Sunadomari Kanemoto*

About the Authors

Richard and Kathy Crane are full time professional *Aikido* Instructors. Both hold the rank of 5th Dan (fifth degree black belt) and are the Chief and Resident Instructors of *Aikido Agatsu Dojos*, an organization of six *Dojos* in Southern New Jersey and the surrounding area.

Agatsu Dojos was established and dedicated in 1976 to the proper impartation of the Traditional *Aikido* practice and principles of *O'Sensei Ueshiba Morihei*. *Aikido In Training* is an extension of that commitment.

The Cranes sincerely hope that *Aikido In Training* will be one more step in the direction of preserving *O'Sensei's* art and spreading the joy of rigorous honest endeavor which is at the heart of the *Aiki* Way.

Other works by the Authors

Aikido In Training: Buki Waza Video Series

Aikido In Training: Tai-Jutsu Video Series

For information write:

Cool Rain Productions P.O. Box 145, Berlin, New Jersey 08009 USA

or

Aikido Agatsu Dojos **31 South White Horse Pike, Stratford, New Jersey 08084 USA**